Other Fromm Paperbacks:

SECRETS OF MARIE ANTOINETTE:
A Collection of Letters
edited by Olivier Bernier

KALLOCAIN: *A Novel*
by Karin Boye

TALLEYRAND: *A Biography*
by Duff Cooper

AMERICAN NOTES: *A Journey*
by Charles Dickens

BEFORE THE DELUGE: *A Portrait
of Berlin in the 1920's*
by Otto Friedrich

THE END OF THE WORLD:
A History
by Otto Friedrich

J. ROBERT OPPENHEIMER:
Shatterer of Worlds
by Peter Goodchild

THE ENTHUSIAST: *A Life
of Thornton Wilder*
by Gilbert A. Harrison

INDIAN SUMMER: *A Novel*
by William Dean Howells

A CRACK IN THE WALL:
Growing Up Under Hitler
by Horst Krüger

EDITH WHARTON: *A Biography*
by R. W. B. Lewis

THE CONQUEST OF MOROCCO
by Douglas Porch

THE CONQUEST OF THE SAHARA
by Douglas Porch

HENRY VIII: *The Politics of Tyranny*
by Jasper Ridley

INTIMATE STRANGERS:
The Culture of Celebrity
by Richard Schickel

BONE GAMES: *One Man's Search
for the Ultimate Athletic High*
by Rob Schultheis

KENNETH CLARK: *A Biography*
by Meryle Secrest

THE HERMIT OF PEKING:
The Hidden Life of Sir Edmund Backhouse
by Hugh Trevor-Roper

ALEXANDER OF RUSSIA:
Napoleon's Conqueror
by Henri Troyat

Flaubert & Turgenev

A friendship in letters

*'We are a pair of moles burrowing away
in the same direction.'*
Turgenev to Flaubert
May 1868

Flaubert
&
Turgenev

A friendship in letters

The complete correspondence

BARBARA BEAUMONT
editor

Fromm International Publishing Corporation
New York

Published in 1987 by Fromm International Publishing Corporation,
560 Lexington Avenue, New York, NY 10022
by arrangement with W. W. Norton & Company, Inc.

Flaubert & Turgenev: A Friendship in Letters
Copyright © 1985 by Barbara Beaumont
Translation, Introduction, Notes

Printed in the United States of America

Contents

Preface

The extant correspondence between Flaubert and Turgenev has not before been published as an exchange of letters in one volume, either in the original French or in any other language. Gérard-Gailly presented Flaubert's half of the correspondence to the French reading public in the 1940s, and some of the letters have appeared in English in anthologies and selections, such as those of Halpérine-Kaminsky, F. Steegmuller, A.V. Knowles and D. Lowe. Details of these and of other related works are given in the Bibliography.

This present edition juxtaposes letter and answer allowing the English reader access to a fuller appreciation of the real depth of friendship and genuine intellectual exchange that linked these two great figures of nineteenth-century fiction.

Introduction

The nature of the correspondence

'there can only be close
friendship and solidarity
between two men when their
intellects have made contact'
De Vogüe, *Le Roman russe*[1]

That the friendship between Flaubert and Turgenev was close and
meaningful is abundantly clear from the two hundred and thirty-odd
letters they exchanged over a period of some seventeen years. Their
relationship was founded on the deep understanding between two
men of the same generation who have undergone essentially compara-
ble aesthetic experiences. It was this common ground that made
contact on an intellectual level easy when they met in the 1860s, the
friendship ending only with the death of Flaubert in 1880. Their
'solidarity' as writers (to use de Vogüe's phrase) stems then from both
the parallel experiences of their first forty years of life and the
convergence of their literary aesthetic: a mutual desire to base their
works on the same principles of impartiality and objectivity.

A high percentage of their exchange of letters has survived, providing valuable insights into both the artistic and private lives of these
two major novelists. At the time of their meeting, both men were
isolated emotionally, and in such circumstances the letter can become
a valuable psychological support and link, and particularly so when
the correspondent turns out to be a sensitive and sympathetic soul.

It is widely accepted that the correspondence of Gustave Flaubert
constitutes one of the most fascinating documents of French literature;
André Gide admitted to having had it at his bedside in place of the
Bible for five years, gaining from its reading 'a reservoir of energy'.
Turgenev also was a talented and prolific correspondent, writing
fluently in French, English and German besides his native Russian.
The letters they wrote to each other vary in length and content, but
their interest is consistent when viewed in the context of the relationship between the two men as a whole. Some are simple notes to
arrange a dinner party or a meeting to discuss literary matters, but

even these reveal the frequency and intimacy of contact between them. Others, often those sent to and from Spasskoye, Turgenev's country estate in southern Russia, contain long passages devoted to their literary projects, their philosophy of life and the contemporary scene in all its aspects, thus reflecting the state of mind and morale of the two writers and their world over a relatively long period of their creative lives. The subjects ranged over during their years of correspondence include the works of Emile Zola, George Sand, Leo Tolstoy, the theatre, the press, the Franco-Prussian War and the beginnings of the Third Republic in France.

Fascinating psychological differences between the two writers emerge from a study of these letters. Thus becomes apparent the value of an exchange between two equals: men of similar age (three years only separated them), profession and standing. Flaubert emerges as the one most singlemindedly committed to literature, his writing occupying his time and energies almost exclusively, with years devoted to the composition of a single book, months to a single chapter. Turgenev on the other hand could, when pressed by his publisher, dash off a short story within the month or finish off a problematic major novel during his summer holiday. He frequently exhorted Flaubert to be less painstaking and laborious over his work, warning him of the dangers of heaviness and pedantry, and even admitting to a certain laziness on his own part.

Flaubert here lives up to his reputation as the hermit of Croisset, preferring by far the calm and solitude of his riverside retreat near Rouen to the world of the Paris salons. His wish was always that Turgenev should come to him at Croisset, where they could be alone together and that he should stay 'for a long time'. In this last respect, he was invariably disappointed, for Turgenev, much more of a natural socialite, enjoyed the larger gatherings, the literary dinners and the musical evenings of the Parisian winter season. Flaubert also reveals himself to be the more emotionally dependent of the two; there is not infrequently an almost whining tone in his refrain 'when shall we see each other . . . when shall I have you all to myself', and a rather childish note (albeit self-consciously so) in his 'write me a long letter, I have been good and deserve favours'. Although, in all fairness, Turgenev must have been a great source of frustration to Flaubert. He repeatedly changed arrangements, broke appointments and made only whirlwind visits to Croisset, never staying for the two weeks begged for by Flaubert year after year. Often Turgenev's apparent lack of constancy was through no fault of his own: he was a frequent victim of violent attacks of gout (although also a noted hypochondriac). But another factor was certainly his own emotional dependence on the singer Pauline Viardot; and Flaubert realised as much, as is clear in a comment made in a letter to his niece Caroline: 'No news whatsoever from the Muscovite. It's strange! Is he ill? . . . After all, perhaps he is too preoccupied with the Viardots.'[2] Nevertheless their relationship reached a marked degree of intimacy during the last ten years of Flaubert's life, and he especially was not afraid to let his emotions run over into his letters. Of his constant impatience to see Turgenev we read:

> Ah! dear friend, how I should love to stretch out alongside you on your great haystacks! That would refresh my sad and singularly weary being . . .
> I embrace you, *burning* with impatience . . .
> I've never felt the need for anyone as much as I feel the need for you . . .[3]

And that Turgenev loved Flaubert dearly is not in doubt; he was the novelist for whom he had the most unreserved admiration and a man with whom he shared a great bond of affection, as he reveals in the letter he wrote to Flaubert's niece on his death:

> the death of your uncle has been one of the things that has most distressed me in the whole of my life, and I can't get used to the idea that I shan't see him again.[4]

History of a friendship

Flaubert and Turgenev met for the first time on 28 February 1863. The critic Charles-Edmond took his Russian friend to dine at Magny's restaurant on the left bank of the Seine. This establishment had become a weekly meeting place for a whole group of writers, artists and intellectuals of all kinds. Others present on that particular evening included, besides Flaubert, the critic Sainte-Beuve and the diarist Edmond de Goncourt. Although this was the first face-to-face meeting between the two novelists, the ensuing exchange of letters shows that each already enjoyed a considerable familiarity with the other's literary work. Flaubert, aged forty-one, was known as the controversial author of *Madame Bovary*, and had recently published *Salammbô*. Turgenev, three years older, and always the more prolific writer had already produced his *Hunting Sketches*, three major novels (*A Nest of the Landed Genry, On the Eve* and *Fathers and Children*), plus a number of short stories and plays.

Turgenev wrote his first letter to Flaubert the very next day, and there followed that spring the first friendly, but politely formal exchange of correspondence. These early letters reveal already a mutual admiration and a clear sympathy.

With the exception of a note of 1866 making arrangements for a dinner party, the correspondence then lapsed for a period of five years. But as this establishes, together with the evidence of letters to mutual friends, contact between the two writers was by no means broken off during this time. In the summer of 1864, for example, Flaubert reported to Charles-Edmond an incident concerning the editor of the *Revue des Deux Mondes* 'that Turgenev told me recently'. And in February of the following year he announced to his niece: 'Today I'm dining at Mme Husson's with Turgenev, Taine and Du Camp.'[6]

In 1868 the exchange of letters got on to a regular footing again during Turgenev's summer sojourn in Baden, and it reflects a growing friendship and community of ideas and interests. In November 1868, Turgenev was to make his first visit to Croisset, spending a Sunday in literary chat with Flaubert. The following day the delighted host wrote to a friend: 'There are few men whose company is more pleasant or whose mind more attractive. What a pity that one never lives with the people one loves.'[7]

It was in the winter season 1868–9 that meetings in Paris between the two writers became frequent, and Turgenev started to attend Flaubert's Sunday afternoon gatherings in his rooms in the rue du Temple. Flaubert's correspondence with George Sand for that winter contains many references to dinners and discussions with Turgenev, and for his part the latter painted a graphic portrait of Flaubert at home in a letter to Claudie, one of the Viardot daughters:

> the great Flaubert, an artist, a painter, he is dressed untidily in a Turkish style – a knitted waistcoat with brown and red stripes – his room is painted red with the doors painted blue with golden crescents on the panels – his face is red also, a prominent stomach, green oriental slippers. Eccentric and *natural* which is more rare! Friendly, very clever, he uses picturesque language; likeable, and I have the impression that he likes me, and that's always nice.[8]

1869 saw the publication of Flaubert's novel *Sentimental Education* which was not received as favourably as he had hoped, the disappointment being all the greater as he had been working on the book for over six years. Turgenev was one of the few *literati* to appreciate the novel's real worth, and he sought to boost Flaubert's flagging morale by sending him copies of favourable reviews from foreign journals, just as he was to do again five years later for *The Temptation of Saint Anthony*.

After the *débâcle* of the Franco-Prussian War and the Commune,

Turgenev, who had been in self-imposed exile in London with the
Viardots, returned in the late summer of 1871 to Paris, which was to
become much more his home base in the following decade. That
winter provided the opportunity to renew contact on a regular basis.
Early in December, Flaubert commented to George Sand that since his
arrival in the capital he had seen no one 'except Turgenev' whom he
found 'more charming than ever'.[9] It was at this time that Turgenev
introduced Flaubert to the Viardot household and he reciprocated by
securing his Russian friend admission into the circle of the Princess
Mathilde, cousin to the Emperor Napoléon III, and whose literary
salon was amongst the most brilliant of the period.

De Goncourt records two notable dinners in the winter of 1872 at
which both Flaubert and Turgenev were present. On 2 March the
diarist, together with Turgenev and Théophile Gautier, dined at
Flaubert's rooms. De Goncourt was delighted with the Russian
writer, 'the amiable barbarian' with thick white hair falling over his
forehead. Over the soup, Turgenev charmed them all with his 'com-
bination of naivety and finesse, his immense and cosmopolitan store-
house of knowledge'. The evening encompassed many subjects of
conversation: comic drama from Aristophanes to Molière; presenti-
ments of death – Théophile Gautier was already ill with heart disease –
and perhaps most significantly, the role of love in the life of the artist.
Turgenev (aged fifty-three) declared himself impotent and completely
incapable of love, seeing this state of affairs as a foretaste of death.
Goncourt and Flaubert riposted that love was a thing of lesser significance for the man of letters, implying a compensation to be found in
the act of artistic creation. But Turgenev stood his ground, declaring
vehemently: 'My life is steeped in feminality. No book, nor anything
else has ever been able to take the place of a woman for me. How can I
explain it? I find that only love produces a certain fulfilment of ones
being, that nothing else can give.' He proceeded to reminisce about a
poor miller's daughter who was once his mistress, and who refused all
money or gifts, except for a bar of soap, in order to make herself
worthy of her lover's caresses. 'There has been nothing in my life to
compare with that moment', concluded Turgenev.[10]

Three weeks later, de Goncourt returned the invitation and the two
novelists dined with him. The host records in detail Turgenev's
portrayal of the Moscow publishing scene, with illiterate publishers
and drunken copy-editors; and he indulged further in rather risqué
accounts of youthful amorous adventures. Interestingly enough, de
Goncourt explains Turgenev's expansiveness by his feeling himself so
completely at ease in that company, amongst friends with whom he
had so much in common, 'so many atoms linked together' in the
more graphic French phrase.[11] In January 1873 Flaubert took a new

apartment in Paris, in the rue Murillo, overlooking the Parc Monceau. This meant that he was living within walking distance of Turgenev, who was lodging with the Viardots in the rue de Douai, just on the other side of the Gare St Lazare. They met often: at the Princess Mathilde's Wednesday salons, at Mme Viardot's Friday musical evenings, but again most frequently at Flaubert's on Sunday afternoons. 'Turgenev visits me most Sundays' he commented in a letter to Mme Régnier of this period, and on the value of his friendship: 'Mme Sand and Turgenev are the only literary friends left to me. But these two are worth a whole host of others, it's true.'[12]

That very spring, the two men made plans to spend Easter together at Nohant, the country house of George Sand in the province of Berry. Towards the end of March Flaubert wrote to Mme Sand: 'The giant Turgenev has just left my house, and we have taken a solemn oath. You shall have us to dinner on 12 April, the day before Easter.'[13] Flaubert kept the appointment, but Turgenev did not arrive until the following Wednesday evening, having missed Tuesday's six-hour reading by Flaubert of his manuscript of *The Temptation of Saint Anthony*. As the hostess records in her diary, the following day, Thursday, was wet and so was spent in literary chat. Later Turgenev read a comic piece and there was singing and dancing with the grandchildren, but Flaubert would keep interrupting, wanting to talk literature the whole time. They left together early on the Saturday; as far as Châteauroux station, they travelled in George Sand's own carriage, philosophising happily, as Flaubert recounts in his thankyou letter.[14] But the remainder of the journey back to Paris, by rail, was less pleasant, as they did not manage to keep a compartment to themselves. Flaubert however, found some consolation in the flask of excellent *eau-de-vie* that Turgenev had with him. 'We both had rather heavy hearts,' he writes, 'we didn't talk and we didn't sleep.'

Some weeks later, the three of them were to meet up again in Paris, where they dined one evening in May, together with Edmond de Goncourt. The occasion was apparently not a success, however, Mme Sand being rather ill humoured and accusing Flaubert of selfish behaviour.

After his usual summer peregrinations through German watering places, Turgenev returned to France and Flaubert managed to keep him at Croisset for three whole days early in October 1873. After the visit, he wrote in delighted terms to his niece:

> My Muscovite left this morning. . . . You can't imagine the extent of his knowledge. He recited extracts from the tragedies of Voltaire and from Luce de Lancival by heart! I think he knows even the

darkest recess of every literature in the world! And he's so modest with it! So cheerful, such an old devil! On Friday I took him to Jumièges but all the rest of the time, we never stopped talking, and I'm frankly exhausted by it. Those were three exquisite days!

I read to him *The Weaker Sex*, my fairy play and the first act of *The Candidate*, together with the plan of this latter. He likes *The Candidate* best; he thinks *The Weaker Sex* will be successful. As for my fairy play, he had a useful criticism, which I shall put into practice. The stock pot [*Saint Anthony*] made him bellow with enthusiasm! He thinks it beats all the rest. But he thinks *The Candidate* will be a good play. This judgement encourages me no end, and I shall start work on it again tomorrow.[15]

Turgenev was to become further involved with *The Candidate* that winter; in December he spent a whole day going through the manuscript with Flaubert after the play's first reading at the Vaudeville Theatre. Carvalho, the manager had asked for some changes to be made, and Turgenev helped work these out. Flaubert wrote to his niece that he had even come back after dinner one evening and they had worked on it together until 1 a.m. Unfortunately the confidence in the play's success that Turgenev had expressed during his stay at Croisset was to prove ill-founded. The play was booed at its first night on 11 March 1874, and Flaubert withdrew it after only four performances, not wishing to submit his actors to further humiliation. The play aimed to reflect the turmoil in political affairs in France since the Franco-Prussian War and is set in a provincial town during an election campaign.

The only reference Turgenev makes to *The Candidate* in his correspondence with others is in a letter to his friend Annenkov written a month after the play's first night. He simply states: 'Flaubert's comedy is decidedly a flop.'[16]

This period was one of the least productive for Turgenev himself; a few short stories, nostalgic in tone, were all that he produced. He was during this time trying to come to grips with his plans for *Virgin Soil*, his last major novel, the writing of which turned out to be more traumatic than any of his earlier works. Flaubert too was naturally discouraged by the lack of success of his own recent works, and he tells of a day in the late summer of 1874 that he and Turgenev spent in commiseration:

The poor old Muscovite has been back for two days and is more ill than ever. I went to see him at Bougival (a dreadful journey as one has to go by omnibus – he has no idea of the sacrifice I made for him) and we spent our time in moaning and groaning about our respective ills. Of course *Bouvard and Pécuchet* dominated the conversation . . .[17]

Bouvard and Pécuchet, conceived as an exposure of public stupidity and narrow-mindedness, was Flaubert's latest literary venture, which was to occupy him on and off until his death.

The winter of 1874–5 found Flaubert and Turgenev both in Paris again, and as in the previous year, they saw a great deal of each other. De Goncourt recounts vividly the discussions at some of the Sunday afternoon gatherings at Flaubert's. One week Turgenev spent the whole session doing extempore translations from Goethe's *Prometheus* and *Satyros*. Flaubert was astounded at his skill and sensitivity as a translator. On another occasion, the subject of conversation was hallucination. Turgenev told how, on going down to dinner one day, he passed the open door of Louis Viardot's room, and caught a glimpse of him at the basin washing his hands, yet on entering the dining room, he found Viardot seated at his usual place. Flaubert for his part explained how, after spending long periods bent over his desk absorbed in work, he always had the feeling, on sitting up straight again, that there was someone standing close behind him.[18] Both writers retained a lifelong fascination with unusual psychological states, where the borders between reality, dream and hallucination become blurred.

The famous 'dîners des cinq' at the Café Riche also date from this period. The five were, besides Flaubert and Turgenev, Emile Zola, Alphonse Daudet and Edmond de Goncourt. The latter describes the group as 'talented people who admire each other' adding 'we should like to make these meetings monthly in future winters'.[19] Daudet had another explanation. In his volume of memoirs he wrote:

It was at this time we had the idea of monthly meetings, where friends would meet for a good meal; they were called 'the Flaubert dinners' or 'the dinners for heckled playwrights'. Flaubert was there on account of the failure of *The Candidate*, Zola with *Bouton de rose*, Goncourt with *Henriette Maréchal*, me for my *Arlésienne*. Girardin wanted to join us, but he's not a writer so we cut him out. As for Turgenev, he gave us his word that he'd been booed in Russia, and as it's a long way, we didn't go and find out.[20]

As a result of the financial ruin brought about by the bankruptcy of his nephew Ernest Commanville in the summer of 1875, Flaubert felt his confidence too shattered to undertake the major project *Bouvard and Pécuchet* as he had intended. And so he cautiously planned to write a single short story of thirty pages based on the legend of St Julian the

Hospitaler, the inspiration coming from a local Norman source, a stained glass window in Rouen cathedral. This was the start of a literary project with which Turgenev was to become intimately involved over the next eighteen months. The one story was to develop into the volume *Three Tales*; and Turgenev was to be responsible for a Russian translation. The idea of foreign publication preceding the publication in Paris was an attempt to increase the revenue from each story, and thus improve the lamentable state of Flaubert's finances. In September 1876 Turgenev was to spend three days at Croisset to discuss the project. (Twice Flaubert wrote anxiously to his niece from Paris ahead of the visit asking her to measure the various beds at Croisset 'in view of his gigantic size'.)

Despite the essentially commercial nature of the translation enterprise, Turgenev does reveal a high opinion of the *Legend of St Julian* in his first mention of it to Stasyulevich in a letter of March 1876: 'I forgot to tell you that Flaubert has written a highly original legend. It delighted me so much that I decided to translate it.'[21] And later he described the third story *Hérodias* to Henry James as being 'of great beauty'.[22]

But these translations were to become ultimately something of a bone of contention between the two writers. For Flaubert, the essential was that his stories should appear promptly in a Russian journal, as he was to receive a premium rate for them if this were their first publication, and obviously he did not wish to delay publication in France, equally for financial reasons. For once he seems to have been more concerned about speed than about quality in a literary venture. Rather than trouble Turgenev with the work of translating all three stories, he urged him to find somebody to do the job 'more or less well'. Turgenev was keen that the translation should be well done, and, what is more, he also knew that these works must bear his own name as translator if the editor of the Petersburg journal the *European Messenger* was to pay the top rate for them. But although full of good intentions concerning this collaborative effort with Flaubert, Turgenev appears to have dragged his feet over his part of the enterprise to such an extent that he was even forced to invent an elaborate complex of lies to cover up the delay. The story he told Flaubert, about having published a declaration that nothing would appear under his name before his novel *Virgin Soil*, was a complete fabrication, to which he also engaged Stasyulevich's complicity in keeping the secret.[23] Indeed Turgenev's correspondence with the editor of the *European Messenger* at this period is full of remarks such as: 'I shall probably send my translation about 13 February', 'I hope still in time for the March issue'. 'I hope to get it to you in time. . . . Despite all my efforts, I haven't finished copying out Flaubert's legend . . .

probably too late for the March issue.'[24] Publication had originally been planned for the preceding November!

Then there was the question of the second tale, *Story of a Simple Soul*, which in fact never appeared in Russian translation. To Stasyulevich Turgenev admits to finding this story of the old servant, who 'concentrates all her affection on a parrot', less successful than the other two, and he also foresaw problems with the imperial censorship over the episode where the heroine 'confuses it [the stuffed parrot] with a manifestation of the holy ghost'.[25] Turgenev had told Flaubert that he had found a Russian lady of letters to translate *A simple Soul*, but whether this also was fabrication is not certain.

The two stories *St Julian* and *Hérodias* finally came out in the April and May 1877 issues of the *European Messenger*. Turgenev wrote a preface for the publication of the first instalment in the form of a letter to the editor of the review. It is here quoted in full:

> Gustave Flaubert, the well-known author of *Madame Bovary*, *Salammbô* and *Sentimental Education*, one of the most remarkable representatives of contemporary French literature, has sent me three stories or 'legends' written by him, *Saint Julian, A Simple Soul*, and *Hérodias*, which are due to come out in Paris at the beginning of May. Struck by the particular beauty of each one, different in each case, I translated two of them, 'Julian' and 'Hérodias', from the manuscript. I offer them to you for publication in the *European Messenger*. These legends may cause some surprise amongst Russian readers, who will not be expecting such from the man who claims to be the leading French realist, having assumed the mantle of Balzac. But I imagine that the brilliant, and at the same time harmonious and well-constructed poetry of these legends will win over the readers and conquer any prejudices. Let them but glance at each one as if it were a poem rendered in prose – which it is.
>
> For my part, I brought to this task all possible skill and experience. It was in fact 'love's labour',* a work of love, may my labour not have been in vain – 'love's labour lost'.*[26]

Turgenev took no payment for his work of translation; he told Stasyulevich that the whole of the fee was to go directly to Flaubert who, meanwhile, was getting rather frustrated at the delays, for which he suspected his friend was at least in part responsible, as he wrote to Caroline in December 1876:

* In English in the original.

The Muscovite has not yet answered me about the date of the Russian publication. How rare a thing a straight line is! What would it cost him to be categorical and do what he had said! But no! He dawdles, he puts it off! Or is it me who's being anti-social?[27]

In Turgenev's defence, though, his friend Pavlovsky paints a much more devoted picture of Turgenev as translator. He wrote in his recollections:

he had translated two of his [Flaubert's] stories . . . with love that verged on passion. He spent a whole month translating each story, spending hours looking for the right phrase. Thus one can say that Flaubert is rendered there as he will never be again in any language.[28]

However a more sober judgement on the quality of these translations of *St Julian* and *Hérodias* is made by the Soviet critic Kleman who undertook a detailed textual comparison of Flaubert's and Turgenev's versions in the 1930s. He found many unexplained variations from the original, and a great deal of looseness. He concluded that despite their intrinsic interest as literary curiosities, 'Turgenev's translations cannot be considered adequate renderings of the original . . . lacking in accuracy [as they do].'[29]

In the winter and spring of 1876 there were many meetings between the two novelists, and Flaubert commented to George Sand that he found Turgenev, one of his Sunday 'habitués' 'nicer than ever', and this in spite then of the contretemps over the *Three Tales*. Eating a bouillabaisse supper seemed to be the favourite formula for a pleasant evening with the five heckled playwrights that year. De Goncourt records a very relaxed evening at Alphonse Daudet's in January, where this fish dish from the host's native Provence was the *pièce de résistance*. Turgenev had come in his slippers, on account of his gout, de Goncourt tells us, and 'Everyone feels, elbow to elbow, amongst sympathetic souls – and one eats better in the company of talented people who respect each other.'[30] In February Turgenev treated them all to a Russian-style meal at Adolphe's restaurant, but they were to become regulars at a little tavern behind the Opéra-Comique. De Goncourt tells of another bouillabaisse evening there on 8 May when, as not infrequently amongst the group of five, the main topic of conversation was women and love. On this occasion there seems to have been a good deal of bragging and exaggeration about sexual exploits, Daudet revealing a need to use foul language and brutality with women, whom he would ideally consume two at a time. Turgenev remained more calm, remarking 'It's curious, I only ever approach a woman with emotion, a feeling of respect and surprise at my good fortune.' Flaubert reminisced about his adventures with a woman 'with an ice-cold backside' in a hut in Upper Egypt, although the others accused him of making it up. De Goncourt concludes:

> Turgenev is a pig whose piggishness is tinged with sentimental-ity. . . . Zola is a vulgar and brutish pig, whose piggishness is now entirely taken up with scribbling. . . . Daudet is a sickly pig, with the passing fancies of a brain where madness could some day enter in. . . . Flaubert is a fake pig, claiming to be a pig and pretending to be one, to be on the same level as the real and genuine pigs, his friends. . . . As for me, I am a pig intermittently, with bouts of swinishness, due to the frustrations of the flesh, frenzied by the spermatic animalcule.[31]

According to de Goncourt, this rather lecherous vein of conversation was to continue to dominate at the dinner parties attended by this little group throughout 1878–9.

Having been able to resume work on *Bouvard and Pécuchet* during 1879, Flaubert kept Turgenev well informed as to progress, or the lack of it; in fact the last year of their correspondence is dominated by the spectre of these two characters and Flaubert's lamentations on the exhausting nature of this literary venture. That the Russian novelist did view this difficult and rather unusual work favourably emerges from a letter to de Goncourt, written after another visit to his friend in May 1879: 'I spent two days at Croisset at Flaubert's. He's quite well, all in all, and his work is coming on. He read me three chapters of it which I liked a lot.'[32] He was to provide further encouragement later that year on what was to turn out to be his last visit to Normandy. Turgenev had made the journey, armed with bottles of champagne, to celebrate Flaubert's fifty-eighth birthday on 12 December. As Flaubert wrote to his niece, Caroline: 'We spent twenty-four delight-ful hours together. What a good fellow and what an artist! He put new heart into me for *Bouvard and Pécuchet*, which I greatly need.'[33]

Turgenev left for Russia early in February 1880; Flaubert had been more anxious than usual about his friend's departure, knowing that he risked having problems of a political nature. The situation in the last years of the reign of Tsar Alexander II was very unstable; political demonstrations and attacks on his life were frequent, and so repressive counter-measures were taken. Turgenev feared that as a noted liberal he might risk being exiled to his estate and banned from foreign travel. Later that month Flaubert wrote to his niece: 'The latest attack on the life of the Tsar worries me, on account of the Muscovite.'[34] He was in fact never to see his beloved Muscovite again; Flaubert died suddenly of a stroke, in his bath, on 8 May 1880. Turgenev was in the depths of Russia at the time, and saw the news printed coldly in the newspapers before the consoling letters of friends could reach him to soften the blow. That the loss of this dear friend had a profound effect on him is echoed many times in the letters he wrote over the following weeks. To Toporov and Stasyulevich he described himself as 'greatly afflicted' and 'unable to write any more'.[35] Revealing also are the comments he made in a letter to Marianne Viardot, his favourite amongst the Viardot daughters:

> The death of Flaubert has afflicted me deeply. After your family and Annenkov, he was, I believe, the man I loved most in the world. . . . And here he is, departed for that land from which no traveller has ever returned. The last time I saw him (at Croisset) he had no presentiment of his approaching end – neither did I – and yet he spoke quite freely about death.[36]

Turgenev was keen to give whatever help possible in order to ensure publication of the last fatal work of Flaubert's *Bouvard and Pécuchet*. The affair was to involve him in a certain amount of unpleasantness with the Commanvilles, Flaubert's heirs. They had entrusted the negotiations with Juliette Adam, editor of *La Nouvelle Revue*, to Turgenev. But Commanville subsequently expressed some dissatisfaction at the terms he had obtained. Turgenev wrote back with some displeasure at the difficult position he had been placed in *vis-à-vis* Mme Adam, and refusing to negotiate further. A contract was eventually signed (only a fragment of the letter from Turgenev to Caroline Commanville in which this is discussed survives) and *Bouvard and Pécuchet* appeared in *La Nouvelle Revue* between 15 December 1880 and 1 March 1881.

Turgenev also became closely involved with the committee for the erection of a monument to Flaubert. He accepted appointment as a vice-president and wrote many letters[37] and paid many calls. As was usual the affair dragged on. De Goncourt records a meeting of the committee in April 1881, but the statue itself, finally commissioned from the sculptor Chapu, was not to be unveiled in Rouen until 1890, seven years after Turgenev's own death.

Influences: the literary masters

The achievement of such a degree of mutual sympathy and understanding between Flaubert and Turgenev during the years of their friendship is easier to understand, and indeed seems almost a logical consequence, if one looks carefully at the earliest period of the two writers' development and literary activity. Such comparisons reveal that both had similar tastes in their favourite reading, especially Byron, Goethe, Shakespeare and Cervantes. Their first literary productions show common influences as well as certain parallels in concept and execution. Indeed as the critic Digeon said, the very first letters exchanged by Flaubert and Turgenev in the early 1860s already give an insight into 'the powerful feeling of shared literary origins'[38] that was to form the basis of their intellectual relationship.

Flaubert's interest in and knowledge of Byron is established from the age of fourteen, for among the juvenilia of 1835 is a *Portrait of Lord Byron*. Although a short and conventional piece, it reveals its young author's fascination with the solitary and contemplative aspects of the poet's character. An active interest in Byron is likewise revealed in Turgenev's earliest surviving literary effort. In later years he was to reminisce about this work in the following terms: 'a fantasy drama in iambic pentameters under the title of *Steno . . .* this impossible work of mine, in which with childish incompetence, I was slavishly imitating Byron's *Manfred*'.[39]

Undoubtedly the powerful individualism of the Byronic hero had its appeal, and his legacy is visible in such early creations as Jules, the hero of Flaubert's first full-length (though unpublished) novel, the 1845 *Sentimental Education*, and in Victor Alekseyevich, the hero of Turgenev's *Parasha* of 1844. With increased maturity, this romantic influence is levelled out, but Turgenev admits to being consoled by reading *Don Juan* in the 1870s, and Flaubert always kept a skull on his mantelpiece, as did Lara and the poet himself.

Goethe too had a strong but also more lasting significance in the development of Flaubert and Turgenev, and throughout their careers they ranked him amongst their 'masters' in literary matters. Flaubert was deeply fascinated by *Faust* from his schooldays onwards. His niece paints a highly romantic picture of her uncle enraptured, reading *Faust I* to the sound of the Easter bells on the Cours de la Reine in Rouen. And Turgenev wrote to a friend during his student days in Berlin in the 1830s: 'I am reading Goethe all the time. This reading strengthens me in these dismal days. What treasure I am constantly finding in his works.'[40] Flaubert's correspondence is liberally sprinkled with maxims and quotations from this master, the phrase 'as old Goethe would say' occurs frequently. For his part, Turgenev often took refuge in the philosophy of Goethe in the face of adversity. After the publication of *Virgin Soil* he wrote, for example: 'In St Petersburg today some people are devouring me, others tearing me apart with their teeth. . . . But the best of luck to them! Goethe was right: it's simple: Man bleibt am Ende was man ist.'[41]

They were clearly attracted to Goethe the man as well as his work, and admired his character in respects such as his disdain for the pettiness of the world. The influence of Goethe is of a more profound nature than that of Byron, not simply a borrowing of romantic colour and types, but rather a process of gradual impregnation with the philosophy of the master, so that although they neither repeated nor imitated Goethe in their mature writing, they none the less never deviated from the path traced out for them by Goethe in their youth. Younger writers were invariably told: 'Read Goethe.'[42]

Shakespeare too occupied a place at the summit of literary achievement in the view of Flaubert and Turgenev. They were equally indignant at his denigration by Zola and the naturalist school. He provides a further example of a literary master discovered by the two writers at an early age, and who was to remain a constant presence in their mature tastes, thus having significance for the development of their own creative imaginations. As for early contact with the works of Shakespeare, Turgenev knew him well enough to undertake translations of parts of *Othello* and *King Lear* in 1836–6. Flaubert's earliest surviving mention of Shakespeare occurs in a letter to Ernest Chevalier, written when he was only thirteen: 'Now I am busy with the plays of old Shakespeare, I'm reading *Othello*.'[43]

In the following decade, Flaubert undertook an especially close study of Shakespeare; his letters of this period are full of references to his awe-inspiring genius. To his mistress Louise Colet he describes in some detail the impact of this genius on his own personality:

> When I read Shakespeare I increase in stature, I become more intelligent and more pure. Having arrived at the summit of one of his works, I feel as if I am on the top of a mountain: everything disappears and all is revealed.[44]

Of all Shakespeare's work, it was the figure of Hamlet that held the greatest fascination for Turgenev, and the Hamlet type is to recur in various guises in many of his own works, for example in the stories 'Khor and Kalinych' and 'Peter Petrovich Karataev' in the *Hunting Sketches*. He also used Shakespearean names in his own titles: 'Hamlet of the Shchigrovsky District', 'King Lear of the Steppe'. In this latter work it emerges that what Turgenev esteemed most in Shakespeare's work was the creation of certain human types. We read, The conversation turned on Shakespeare, on his types, and how profoundly and truly they were taken from the very heart of humanity. We admired particularly their truth to life, their actuality.'[45]

Flaubert and Turgenev also shared a common fascination for that great European literary figure Don Quixote, as well as frequent use in their own work of what has been described as the Don Quixote style of novel, in which the hero is portrayed as an adventurer, whose travels form the framework for its action.

In 1860 Turgenev delivered a lecture entitled *Hamlet and Don Quixote* in which he revealed his own division of humanity into two basic types, which he identified with each of these literary heroes. For Turgenev the essential distinction is whether one searches for fulfilment within or without of one's *self*; whether like Don Quixote one seeks for something 'higher than the ego', an external faith in something outside of one's own being, or whether, like Hamlet, one subjects everything 'to the analysis of thought' and is essentially, then, an egoist.[46]

Flaubert, who went as far as to say 'I recognize all my origins in the book that I knew by heart before I could read: *Don Quixote*',[47] surely comes closest to the spirit of Cervantes' work in his last novel *Bouvard and Pécuchet*, both in characterisation and on the thematic level. For there is much in the presentation of the 'two old fellows' that recalls the relationship between the Don and Sancho Panza, and collectively they can be seen as modern Don Quixotes, for the common aspiration of Bouvard and Pécuchet is to search for universal knowledge and truth, which they hope to achieve through all their various researches. And in spite of their repeated and bitter failures, they never lose faith in the eventual realisation of their ideal. Like the hidalgo, they simply pick themselves up and begin again.

It emerges then that the tastes of Flaubert and Turgenev coincided as far as major literary preferences were concerned. They also had similar likes and dislikes amongst writers who figured less prominently. For example, Rabelais and Montaigne were jointly admired, whereas Balzac was something of a *bête noire* for both. Flaubert's caustic quip is famous: 'What a man Balzac would have been, if only he had known how to write.'[48] For his part Turgenev writes: 'nothing by Balzac, of whom I have never been able to read ten pages together, this writer is so foreign and antipathetic to my nature'.[49]

Thus for Flaubert and Turgenev, their early readings in the masters they admired led to the assimilation into their own creative imaginations of a common stock of characters, literary types and ideas.

The common ground: themes and responses

Love, women and happiness

By the time Flaubert and Turgenev met in 1863, although both only in their early forties, the great moments of passion in their lives were over, and each had arrived at a form of resignation as far as love and the search for happiness through relationships with women were concerned.

Flaubert had had his youthful infatuation with Élisa Schlésinger, met during seaside holidays at Trouville, and his turbulent affair with the tenacious poetess Louise Colet. Turgenev's relationship with Mme Pauline Viardot had reached a crisis of passion in 1850, and now after a break, relations had resumed, but on a different footing. Turgenev was henceforward to assume no more than the role of family friend, a kind of adopted uncle to the Viardot children, although he was accepted back under the conjugal roof, and he lived with them in a *ménage à trois* until his death. He preferred this arrangement to seeking a new amorous involvement with a woman free to marry. In fact neither Flaubert nor Turgenev was to embark on any other serious relationship with a woman, although both corresponded on a regular basis with a number of women, often literary ladies – Mlle Leroyer de Chantepie in the case of Flaubert and the Countess Lambert in the case of Turgenev.

Throughout the greater part of their mature years, both writers remained faithful to a faded ideal of love; faithful in so far as they never married and in so far as their relationships with other women were insignificant in comparison. This led to a marked bitterness in their view of the role and functioning of love; this disillusionment is apparent in both their literary works and their letters. Flaubert, for example, offered the following advice to his friend Emmanuel Vasse:

> Stay always as you are, don't get married, don't have children, get as little emotionally involved as possible, give the least hold to the enemy.
> I've seen what they call happiness at close quarters and I looked at its underside; to wish to possess it is a dangerous mania.[50]

Through this view, Flaubert seems to have arrived at the more general philosophical conclusion that happiness is the enemy of beauty in art. This was a lesson he tried to teach the wilful Louise Colet: 'If you try to seek for Happiness and Beauty both at the same time, you will achieve neither the one nor the other, for the latter comes only through sacrifice.'[51]

Turgenev seems to have held largely parallel views on marriage according to the reminiscences of a friend to whom he confided:

> It is not a good thing for an artist to marry. As the ancients used to say, if you serve a Muse, you must serve her and no one else. An unhappy marriage may perhaps contribute to the development of talent, but a happy one is no good at all.[52]

Such sentiments find their echo over and over again in the literary works of the two novelists. In Flaubert's early unpublished novel *November* the prostitute Marie refers to love as 'an illusion which exists only in my heart and yet that I want to hold in my hands.' And this remains a central dilemma for many of the major characters of his subsequent works: Emma Bovary, Salammbô and Frédéric Moreau all fall victim to the same illusory happiness, each suffering in his or her own way from 'something that was lacking, awaiting endlessly I know not what that never came'.[53]

The critic Irving Howe[54] has remarked that in Turgenev's novels the sexual impulse is seldom allowed to reach any of the normal resolutions, and for this reason he goes as far as to accuse Turgenev of sabotage, sabotage of the possibility of a happy sexual relationship in his works: for Elena, Lavretsky, Litvinov and others.

Repeatedly in their works (*Fathers and Children, On the Eve, Rudin, Madame Bovary, Sentimental Education*) Flaubert and Turgenev present a picture of dashed aspirations and renunciation of the quest for love. Sexual relationships are never free from the connotation of guilt; they stress the treacherous nature of happiness and consistently portray love as a form of bondage.

The Temptation of Saint Anthony

In the winter of 1874, Flaubert finished work on *The Temptation of Saint Anthony* (a subject he had originally worked on as early as 1849) and sold the manuscript to the publisher Charpentier. Turgenev was intimately involved with this work both during its composition and after its publication. Flaubert reported to George Sand on their collaborative efforts:

> I spent a good day with Turgenev yesterday and read him the 115 pages of *Saint Anthony* that are written. . . . What a listener, and what a critic! He staggered me with the depth and crispness of his judgements. If only all those who mess about with books could have heard him, what a lesson! He misses nothing. At the end of a section of a hundred lines, he can remember a weak adjective; he made two or three exquisite suggestions on points of detail for *Saint Anthony*.[55]

Why should Turgenev have felt so involved with this most difficult and least accessible work of Flaubert? And this even to the extent in his letters of referring to the work as Anthony, and asking questions that would seem to refer to a person, rather than a literary work. Part at least of the explanation can surely be found in the fact that *Saint*

Anthony was a subject that had tempted Turgenev himself in earlier years. There survives a work of his youth in which he also tried to put the story of the saint into dramatic form. The appeal of the story is obvious: the saint's quest for a perfect understanding of the nature of existence, the metaphysical anguish of his temptation, and the chance to explore unusual psychological states. The central situation in both of their versions of *The Temptation of Saint Anthony*, with a hero thirsting for knowledge and fulfilment, confronted by a temptor who wafts him through time and space and uses sexual attraction as a powerful weapon, is reminiscent of Goethe's *Faust*. Byron's presence is felt in the colour, extravagance and ostentatious romanticism of the two *Temptations*, as well as in the strong individualism of their heroes.

As early as November 1873, Turgenev approached Stasyulevich with a view to securing eventual Russian publication for Flaubert's work, and in January of the following year he announced: 'I have some pleasant news to tell you: my friend Flaubert (the author of *Madame Bovary* etc.) has finally decided to publish his novel *The Temptation of Saint Anthony* . . . one of the most remarkable works of contemporary literature.'[56] Plans went ahead for translation and publication. In January Turgenev sent the first sixty-four pages to St Petersburg, negotiated a price of 125 francs per sheet, and began to write an introduction himself. As far as translation was concerned, Turgenev begged Stasyulevich: 'Please let the translator be of the first rank. Flaubert's syllables are as if chiselled in marble. Let us Russians acquit ourselves honourably.'[57] Turgenev was aware, however, that there might be problems: 'I fear that in a few places censorship . . . will be necessary, and the translator will have to be rather clever to avoid the complicated bits.'[58] After seeing the first instalment Stasyulevich was having serious doubts as to the viability of the work in Russia. Turgenev did not give up so easily. In February he wrote: 'Is there really a danger – and if there is, isn't it possible to avoid it? Flaubert understands the need for cuts and agrees as long as the general tone and meaning aren't affected. . . . In any case, don't give it to strangers to read.'[59] The plan for the translation was ultimately abandoned, without it having been formally banned. The French edition was freely on sale in St Petersburg in the summer of 1874. The only trouble was that nobody bought it; 'a terrible fiasco' as Turgenev reported to Mme Viardot. He was, naturally enough, keen to protect Flaubert from this awful truth; he wrote to Zola: 'The Russian public has not been tempted by his *Anthony* which was not even banned. This fact must be kept from him.'[60]

There survives, amongst Turgenev's Parisian papers, the rough draft of the introduction he planned for Flaubert's *Saint Anthony*. He refers to the work as 'remarkable' and certain to appeal to 'all those who are truly interested in the progress and development of the human mind' – an ambitious claim.[61]

Turgenev was indefatigable in his efforts to promote this work. He did not confine himself to the potential market in Russia, but took on almost the whole of Europe. He acted virtually as Flaubert's literary agent, providing Charpentier with a list of critics for the top journals to whom review copies must be sent. He backed this up by writing himself to all of his contacts in Germany, Austria and England. He repeatedly describes the book as 'highly original', 'most remarkable', 'exceptional'.[62]

Flaubert was deeply touched by Turgenev's attentiveness in trying to ensure the success of his work. He commented to George Sand: 'Good old Turgenev . . . sent me a favourable review of *Saint Anthony* from Berlin. It's not the article that gives me pleasure, but rather him. I saw a lot of him this winter and I like him more and more.'[63]

By the end of the year, Turgenev had had to face up to the fact that despite his own initial enthusiasm and the exceptional nature of the work in his view, *St Anthony* was, as far as the critics and the reading public were concerned, inaccessible and hence a failure. He wrote in rather disillusioned tones to his friend Julian Schmidt, the German literary critic: 'As far as *The Temptation* is concerned, unfortunately you are right and it must be admitted that this remarkable book is essentially in fact difficult to read and barbaric.'[64]

Politics and the contemporary scene

The role that Flaubert and Turgenev adopted *vis-à-vis* politics was essentially that of observer. Neither was active in the political field, and neither found any one political party or doctrine that he could support whole-heartedly. Yet they could not remain oblivious or indifferent to the major events of their times. As Turgenev remarked to Flaubert, 'we can't help groaning and uttering oh! and ah!'

None the less the central idea of liberty remained dear to them throughout their lives. For Flaubert, even as a boy liberty was an important concept, as he wrote to his childhood friend Alfred Le Poittevin: 'After all, what do I need, isn't it liberty?' And he referred to the censor as 'that infamous ravisher of our public liberties'.[65]

As a young man, Turgenev was much more politically aware than Flaubert, and this virtually by the very fact of his Russian nationality. In Russia at this time, it was impossible for any young intellectual to be unaware of the injustices and abuses of the social and political system. And since Gogol had defined a social role for Russian litera-ture, the efforts of young writers tended in that direction, and as

Pavlovsky wrote, Turgenev 'was keen to be seen as the standard bearer of liberal ideas'.[66]

The abortive revolutions of 1848 were the first major international events to strike the political consciousness of the two young writers, both in their twenties at the time. Both rushed to the scene of events in Paris in February of that year as soon as they heard of the insurrection; yet neither stepped outside of the role of observer, and disappointed ones at that, not finding in these events the expected source of inspiration. They shed no tears over the end of Louis-Philippe's reign, but were soon to be disappointed in the Second Republic's inability to establish an orderly and effective regime. Turgenev wrote to Pauline Viardot in disgust at the disturbances he witnessed at the Assemblée Nationale on 15 May. And by the time of the workers' uprising in June, Turgenev and Flaubert were thoroughly disillusioned, the latter didn't even bother to make the journey from Rouen to see what was happening.

Neither writer was able to bring himself to comment on directly or even reflect the events of 1848 in his literary works in the period immediately following the revolution. Yet both did ultimately return to the subject, making quite extensive use of their own experiences of that year in their writing. The revolution of 1848 plays a central role in Flaubert's *Sentimental Education* of 1869, and also figures in *Bouvard and Pécuchet*. Turgenev deals with it in his short stories 'The Man in Grey Spectacles' and 'My Mates Sent Me'; he also brings it in to the story of Rudin, in the second epilogue. It would seem then that the events of 1848, and the ensuing disappointment at the fall of the young republic, and the creation of the Second Empire under Napoleon III, constituted a considerable emotional shock for both Flaubert and Turgenev, and that they needed time and historical perspective before they could handle this material rationally and objectively and put it into artistic form.

After 1848, pessimism is the most general and typical characteristic of the views of Flaubert and Turgenev concerning politics. They no longer expected rational solutions to the problems of the world. They came more and more to reproach the educated classes for their apathy and lack of foresight in their failure to reform from above, before the fateful beginning of a process of change from below. Such was the essential message of Turgenev's *Hunting Sketches* and he spelt it out again unmistakably in his novel *Smoke* of 1867: 'in the course of ten centuries, Russia has produced nothing of her own. We educated people are poor stuff. . . . But wait . . . look at that peasant. . . . That's where it will all come from.'[67] Flaubert's condemnation of the educated classes is at its most vociferous in his famous 'Letter to the Municipal Council of Rouen'.[68] Here he speaks of the end of the bourgeoisie as a virtual certainty, destined to meet the same fate as the aristocracy in 1789, unless it can remedy the situation urgently: 'Enlighten yourself, enlightened classes! With all your capital and your wisdom, you can't found an association to rival the International!'[69]

Both Flaubert and Turgenev were opposed to socialism as it manifested itself in the 1860s and 1870s. Essentially they opposed the socialists on the grounds of their utilitarianism and their authoritarianism. They also found the link between socialism and the church unacceptable; Turgenev referred to 'this unnatural alliance, capable only of breeding monsters'[70] and Flaubert maintained that 'socialism has been ruined by mysticism. . . . I find an enormous amount of Christianity in socialism.'[71] And from his strictly non-religious standpoint this was a bad thing. Turgenev concurred: 'I want truth and not salvation; I expect it from my intellect and not from grace.'[72]

When the Franco-Prussian War broke out in the summer of 1870, Flaubert and Turgenev shared the feeling that France was in a false position and needed in some sense to be punished for the follies of the Second Empire. Turgenev was in Baden Baden at the outbreak of war, living near the Viardots who had chosen a kind of semi-exile during the 1860s, as political opponents of Napoleon III's regime. He had no doubt whatsoever about which side he was on in this confrontation. He was perhaps most outspoken in his pro-Prussian sentiments in his letters to his German speaking friends. In August 1870 he wrote to Ludwig Friedländer:

> I don't need to tell you that I am whole-heartedly on the German side. Truly this is a war of civilisation against barbarism – but not in the sense these French gentlemen intend it. Bonapartism *must* be done away with, whatever the cost.[73]

However non-patriotic and non-nationalistic Flaubert liked to think himself, it was naturally hard for him to adopt a specifically pro-Prussian standpoint, but he saw clearly enough the wrong on the French side. In a letter to his niece at the time of the emperor's flight he commented: 'We had a fine lot of clowns to govern us. We must admit!'[74] And on his return from a visit to Paris where the war mongering had appalled him, he wrote to George Sand: 'Perhaps this race deserves to be punished, and I fear that it will be. . . . What upsets me about this war is that the Prussians are right!   Oh! I wish I were dead so as not to have to think about it all any more.'[75]

In Baden Turgenev was well placed near to the theatre of war. He was able to send detailed letters on the progress of events to his friends in Russia, notably Annenkov. Several of these were passed on to the editor of the *St Petersburg Bulletin* and published as war reports.

As the war dragged on and the Prussians increased their incursions into and occupation of French territory, Turgenev's attitude modified somewhat. To Ludwig Pietsch, although still maintaining that a French victory would have been a defeat for freedom, he made the following reproach: 'but you didn't have to burn Strasbourg. That was clumsy in the extreme and counter productive.'[76] And a month later he wrote to his brother with the conviction that: '(a) Paris will undoubtedly be cruelly bombarded. (b) Alsace will undoubtedly remain part of Germany. (c) The war will continue *for a long time* and will be hideous.'[77]

In November Turgenev exiled himself to London to join the Viardots and it became Flaubert's turn to experience the war at closer quarters. As the Prussians approached Rouen, his feelings also changed. With the prospect of imminent occupation he could no longer conceive that right might be on the Prussian side. He felt old 'as if over eighty' and depressed: 'Can one believe in progress and civilisation with all that's happening? What use is science then? Since this race, full of learned men is guilty of abominations worthy of the Huns and worse.'[78]

The Prussians occupied Rouen in mid-December and Croisset was commandeered as a billet for three officers, seven soldiers and six horses. Flaubert had to admit that they behaved reasonably well; there was a little petty pilfering, but the house was not greatly damaged. None the less he felt the humiliation of it greatly. The sight of Prussian helmets on his own bed was almost too much for him; he found lodgings for himself and his mother in Rouen. His study was respected and he himself had taken the precaution of burying a large parcel of manuscripts in the garden before the Prussians' arrival!

Flaubert was in Brussels visiting the Princess Mathilde in exile when the Commune was declared in Paris in March 1871. He was appalled by what he heard of it: censorship of the press and executions without trial. 'What savages! Poor France will never drag itself out of the Middle Ages, clinging to the gothic idea of a commune.'[79]

Turgenev's reaction was essentially parallel to that of Flaubert; he considered the Commune to be inept and an entirely inappropriate turn of events for France at this time. She should have been showing a united front to the Prussian enemy, rather than tearing herself apart with civil strife. He commented to Pauline Viardot: 'Oh poor unhappy France! What an abyss she has fallen into' and 'what will become of France . . . the nation we all loved so much?'[80] Flaubert would certainly have concurred in the sentiments Turgenev expressed to Valentine Delessert, feeling that a new and alien age had started:

'Decidedly, is it the world that we knew and lived in that is destroying itself?'[81]

These events of 1870–71 served only to confirm the disappointments already experienced in 1848. And as the decade progressed, Flaubert and Turgenev expected nothing good from the Third Republic. The latter deplored its tendency to military dictatorship under Macmahon; Flaubert could no longer be amazed at anything. Politics was just one more manifestation of human stupidity, *'la bêtise humaine'*.

Another parallel experience in the context of political views is the lack of popularity, at the time of publication, of those works of Flaubert and Turgenev which deal with questions of actuality. It was in fact their refusal to take sides in political issues that prevented both authors from enjoying a full measure of success. In *Fathers and Children*, for example, Turgenev strove to be scrupulously fair to both generations, but only succeeded in antagonising both. Similarly, Flaubert's strictly non-partisan approach to the events of 1848 in *Sentimental Education* offended both right and left. And the failure of his play *The Candidate* can be attributed to the same cause.

Ultimately it is the changeability of their artistic temperament that foils all attempts to place Flaubert and Turgenev in any political category. To judge from the recollections of their contemporaries this volatility was a notable feature. Pavlovsky wrote: 'Like all artists, Turgenev strictly speaking didn't have any political opinions. Edgy and easily worked up, he could belong at two hours' interval to parties of opposite extremes. Independent minded on principle moreover, he was also in reality.'[82] Princess Mathilde's memories of Flaubert are essentially parallel: 'He had no political convictions. One minute he would be demanding repressive measures, the next he would be finding them all intolerable. . . . Thus one evening at dinner he declared to us: I am an underminer of all governments of whatever complexion, I would like to destroy them all.'[83]

Pessimism

> 'He [Turgenev] had in
> common with Flaubert a
> pessimism based on a feeling of
> the futility of the modern
> world.'
> Paul Bourget[84]

It would be unrealistic to think of either Flaubert or Turgenev as a 'happy' man. Although happiness is a theme they explored a good deal in their works, they were for the most part obliged to conclude that this ideal was unobtainable, not only for themselves, but for mankind in general, and this in both the private and public spheres of existence. As life progressed, these sentiments were to become intensified and to crystallise into a pessimism which they were to take with them to the grave, and which is amply echoed in the letters they exchanged in the last decade of their lives.

Early contact with romantic literature's melancholy heroes pursued by fate, yet unlike the Romantics unable to find pastoral consolations in nature; disappointment in love at an early age; progressive disillusionment with the political scene: such were the elements that contributed to the formation of this bleak outlook.

Turgenev's short piece *Enough!* is an interesting case to consider, as it is an intensely personal expression of the black sentiments that accumulated in his experience during the 1850s, and he was working on it at the time he met Flaubert in 1863. He certainly knew at least the principal tenets of Schopenhauer's philosophy by this time, and this probably helped him to formulate more precisely his analogous personal feelings. *Enough!* falls into two sections; the first twelve fragments are highly subjective and in part autobiographical, evoking a former passion and its inevitable disappointment. The second part deals with wider philosophical issues, based on a view of nature as supremely hostile. The artist's greatest reproach to nature is that she is eternal and self-renewing, whereas man's life is only transient – like a dance of flies in the sunlight. He regrets man's inability to progress by learning from his mistakes or to profit from the models and lessons of literature: two thousand years ago, Aristophanes chided man for the same faults we see comitted today, and the lessons of such figures as Hamlet and King Lear seem to have had no salutary effect. The concluding sentence of these 'fragments from the notes of a dead artist' is in English: 'The rest is silence.'[85]

On a philosophical level, it is possible to compare this little work of Turgenev with Flaubert's final and unwieldy novel *Bouvard and Pécuchet*, with which Turgenev was indeed himself closely involved. It presents Flaubert's blackest picture of failed aspirations. The two eponymous heroes search constantly after intellectual progress. By the end of the book, they have laboured through the following branches of learning:

Agriculture, arboriculture and formal gardening.
Chemistry, medicine, astronomy, archaeology, geology.
History, prehistory, philosophy of history
Politics
Gymnastics

Mesmerism, magnetism, spiritualism
Metaphysics, Christianity, Buddhism
Pedagogy

But in line with Turgenev's reflections in *Enough!* they learn nothing from their experiences. The work is, as Thorlby says, 'an immensely complex and comprehensive mathematical formula which makes everything equal zero'.[86] This effect is achieved by the eternal new beginnings that the characters make in their researches; their successive infatuations with new subjects, their enthusiasm and their hard work end, without exception, in failure.

And in the major novels of the two writers, hardly ever do we find positive achievement or lasting happiness; so many of their characters die a premature and futile death: Emma Bovary, Salammbô, Rudin, Insarov, Bazarov. The novel of personal failure is virtually a sub-genre in the work of Flaubert and Turgenev. There are, in fact, close conceptual parallels between such apparently different novels as *Rudin* and *Madame Bovary*, for in each the central character lives in a world of illusion and frustrated ambitions, ending in early death and the wasting of all their energies.

The works of Flaubert and Turgenev converge then in the expression of a profound pessimism, revealed in the recurrence of parallel themes: the transience of life, the power of death and fate, and the inevitability of suffering in all forms of conscious existence.

Work

Face to face with the apparent futility of life, Flaubert and Turgenev both came to the realisation that it was vital to find one positive sphere of activity in one's existence. Flaubert sums up the potential solution to the problem: 'It's through working that I manage to silence my natural melancholy.'[87] Work could come to represent a significant achievement in an otherwise negative world, and thus prevent life from degenerating totally into meaninglessness.

The lesson that life is hard work is one that is repeatedly learnt by the heroes of Turgenev's novels, and this usually after some sentimental disappointment. He sums up this view of life on the last page of his short story 'Faust':

In conclusion I say to you, one conviction I have gained from the experience of the last years . . . life is hard labour. Renunciation, continual renunciation, that is its secret meaning, its solution. Not the solution of cherished dreams and aspirations.[88]

And Flaubert's Saint Anthony, even in the original version of 1849 learns the value of work. His initial monologue refers to 'langour, desperate impotence' but then a moment of revelation comes and life is made bearable by the message the saint receives: 'One day I heard a voice that said to me: Work! And since that time I work away furiously at these foolish occupations which fill up my existence.'[89]

In their personal lives, it was naturally literary work that fulfilled this life-preserving function for Flaubert and Turgenev. As a young man the former had written to Alfred Le Poittevin:

> I continue my painstaking work, like the good labourer, who with his sleeves rolled up and his hair covered in sweat, hammers on his anvil without worrying about whether its raining or windy.[90]

And later we see that for him there are close parallels between the life of the writer and the monastic vocation: 'I love my work with a frenzied and perverted love, like an ascetic loves the hair shirt that scratches his stomach.'[91] It is well known that his devotion to the task of composition was total and selfless; his research was enormous in volume and range. He spared nothing in his grapplings with 'the torments of style', the very putting together of sentences.

Turgenev was also a painstaking and methodical worker; André Mazon, in his study of his manuscripts, contrasts Turgenev's quiet organisation of his work 'as an orderly man, with regular habits' with the hasty feverish composition of Balzac or Dostoevsky. Like Flaubert, he accepted the necessity to rework things many times to achieve the required effect, writing to his friend Aksakov: 'If Pushkin and Gogol had to start their work afresh ten times, how many times will we mediocre souls have to re-do ours.'[92]

Flaubert came to wonder if this very skill of the artist in composition did not have an intrinsic value of its own. While working on his *Legend of Saint Julian* he wrote to George Sand: 'I ask myself whether a book, independently of what it has to say, cannot produce the same effect. Is there not, in the precision of composition, the rarified nature of its component parts, the polish on its surface, the harmony of the whole, an intrinsic virtue?'[93]

The moral of the ending of Voltaire's *Candide* ('That is all very well . . . but we must cultivate our garden') is one that Flaubert esteemed highly. To de Goncourt he described Voltaire's rejection of speculation in favour of activity as 'the greatest lesson in wisdom that exists'.[94] And indeed Candide's words wre a favourite quotation of Flaubert's.

Turgenev, in his prose poem *The Cup*, would seem also to have assimilated Voltaire's lesson as it affects the life of the artist; the writer's efforts in the domain of form and style being his own way of cultivating his garden:

> My feelings are all gloom and desolation. And yet I go out of my way to give polish and beauty to them; I search for images and comparisons; I like my phrases to be well constructed and take a special pleasure in the ring and harmony of words.[95]

Despite the fundamental pessimism of Flaubert and Turgenev's world view, there is a glimmer of a hope of salvation in the achievement of a well-ordered and hard-working life. As Flaubert wrote: 'I don't believe that happiness is possible, but I think tranquillity is.'[96]

Aesthetics and assessments

The close personal relationship between Flaubert and Turgenev was undeniably an important element in the last decade of the life of each man, but what drew them together above all else was their work, the bond of the writer's craft. Barely a month after his first meeting with the Russian writer, Flaubert wrote to him: 'How many things that I have felt and experienced myself have I found in your work! And he readily admitted that Turgenev was the only one of his friends fully to understand and share his views on art and beauty, referring to him as 'the only man in existence really devoted to literature'.[97] The feeling was mutual, Flaubert being for Turgenev the master in all matters literary, and whatever 'Flaubertus dixit' was the final word. Both were convinced of the profound understanding between them, and they often referred to the 'total sympathy' which seemed to exist between their two minds.

On the whole, both Flaubert and Turgenev must be described as realist novelists, if we accept as the basis of this term René Wellek's definition 'the objective representation of contemporary social reality'.[98] As a young man, Flaubert wrote to his friend Louis Bouilhet on the problematical subject of *what* to write about: 'To return to the ancient world: it's been done already; to the middle ages: it's been done already. There remains the present.'[99] Yet he felt unsure and unhappy with the modern world: 'the base is shaky; where can one put down one's foundations?' Although his vast correspondence contains expressions of disgust at the subject of virtually all his major works, eventually three out of four mature novels, and one out of three short stories, wer to be reflections of the present, i.e. nineteenth-century France.

Turgenev also determined early in his career that he should deal with the present in his literary works. In 1845 he wrote an article for a French magazine on contemporary Russian literature where he stated the opinion that: 'To reproduce the life of the present day in all the variety it presents has become the common aim of the efforts of all writers.'[100]

Neither man wished to be classified as part of a literary movement or school however, nor to base his works on any kind of doctrine or system of philosophy. Although admirers of Tolstoy, both had reservations about the third volume of *War and Peace*, which pinpoint nicely the closeness of their literary judgements, and also underline the gulf that separates them from other nineteenth-century novelists such as Balzac, Dostoevsky and Zola, besides Tolstoy himself. Flaubert complains that in this final volume 'we see the man, the author, the Russian', whereas the two preceding volumes of *War and Peace* had been purely and simply reflections of 'Nature and Humanity', thus gaining Flaubert's highest approval: '*sublime*'. Turgenev wrote back delighted to find that his friend concurred in his own views: 'you've put your finger on the weak spot; he also has built himself a system of philosophy which is at the same time mystical, childish and presumptuous, and has terribly spoilt his third volume'. For his own part Turgenev declared to his friend Milyutina: 'I do not believe in any absolutes or systems.'[101] And Flaubert wrote in similar vein to Mlle de Chantepie, rejecting *a priori* all literary movements and revealing a pragmatic approach in philosophy: 'How can we with our limited senses and finite understanding arrive at absolute knowledge?'[102]

Their approach to the function of reality for the artist is also broadly parallel. It should be no more than a starting point for the novelist, who must not try to reproduce the real world, detail by detail as a photographer does. Turgenev criticised George Sand's *François le Champi* in the following terms: 'Perhaps she incorporates rather too many peasant expressions; from time to time it makes her story rather affected. Art is not a daguerreotype, and such a great master as Mme Sand could have dispensed with such a caprice.'[103] In a letter to Turgenev of 28 October 1876, Flaubert made a similar point apropos of Zola's use of language in *L'Assommoir*:

Let louts speak in loutish language, fine, but why should the author share their style? And he thinks it's ever so clever, without realising that by this very quirk, he's reducing the impact of the effect he seeks to create.

They did not wish, then, to copy reality, but to make a choice from among the disparate elements of the real world. What they objected to in naturalism was precisely the lack of this kind of selection on the part of the artist. In the view of Flaubert and Turgenev, the writer should above all *present* aspects of reality to the reader. He should aim to show and demonstrate 'the things of this world' but should make no *explicit* judgement about them. Flaubert summed up neatly this view of the artist's function when he wrote to Louise Colet: 'Let us blame nothing, let us sing of everything, let us *show* things, not discuss them',[104] and ten years later to Mlle Leroyer de Chantepie: 'the greatest geniuses . . . the elder sons of God . . . have all been cautious to do nothing but *present* things'.[105]

This is essentially the artistic method employed by Turgenev in his *Hunting Sketches*. The inhumanity of the serf-based economy is made crystal clear in stories such as 'Yermolay and the Miller's Wife' and 'Ovsyanikov the Freeholder'. Yet nowhere does Turgenev as author intervene in the fiction explicitly to condemn the system or pass judgement on the landowners. These stories reveal precisely the qualities that Flaubert found sadly lacking in Harriet Beecher Stowe's account of slavery in *Uncle Tom's Cabin*. He described this work as 'a narrow book. It's written from a moral and religious point of view: it should have been done from a humanitarian point of view.' It is just this human aspect of the question that Turgenev stresses, presenting the Russian *muzhik* as a sensitive and dignified being in stories such as 'Khor and Kalinych' or 'Raspberry Spring'. Flaubert took great exception to the intrusions of the author in *Uncle Tom's Cabin*: 'The author's reflections irritated me the whole time. Does one need to make reflections on slavery? Show it, that's all.'[106] And Turgenev simply presents a social evil to his reader, leaving to him the responsibility for drawing conclusions.

Self-effacement and consistent elimination of the person of the author were what Flaubert and Turgenev consciously strove for in their writing. The former's view was that the writer's relationship to his work should be essentially the same as God's relationship to his universe: 'present everywhere, yet visible nowhere' and that also like God, he should 'create and keep quiet'.[107] Similarly Richard Freeborn describes Turgenev's method in *Fathers and Children* as 'that of a chronicler, withholding himself from the fiction to an unprecedented degree'.[108] Paul Bourget reminisces about a metaphor Turgenev himself used to convey his efforts to achieve this God-like stance in literature: 'He used to say . . . that his main concern, when he was writing a novel, was to cut the umbilical cord between his characters and himself.'[109] Perhaps as a by-product of this search for objectivity in art, both writers reveal a considerable amount of modesty as far as their literary careers are concerned. Flaubert put his notion of 'conceal your life' into practice in his everyday existence as well as in literature. The most striking example was when *Le Figaro* published the news of his broken leg in 1879. Far from being gratified at the expression of concern for his well-being, he took it virtually as an insult. Similarly Turgenev found articles about himself distasteful. He had agreed to let Maupassant write one about him in a series 'Great Foreign Writers', but he changed his mind: 'Having thought about it, I would rather you didn't write this article about me. You would do it admirably with tact and balance; but I'm afraid that people would find it – excuse the phrase – a kind of friendly advertising.'[110]

Although Flaubert and Turgenev considered reality as no more than a springboard for the artist, they were both concerned to base their literary works on observation and research. Flaubert advised Louise Colet in the following terms: 'Have the model in view all the time, and nothing else.'[111] And when writing *A Simple Soul* he admitted: 'I have a stuffed parrot on my table, so as to be able to "paint" from nature.'[112] And his research is legendary: his journey to Tunisia to observe the site of Carthage for *Salammbô*, the years spent building up the dossiers for *Bouvard and Pécuchet*. In their detail and meticulousness, these give the impression of being the groundwork for an encyclopaedia rather than a novel.

Turgenev also relied greatly on observation for the characters and settings of his novels, and although he lived in western Europe a good deal of the time, hardly a year went by in which he did not make an extended visit to Russia 'to breathe in his native air' as he liked to say. Indeed Turgenev, like Flaubert, uses as settings for his novels only places known personally to him. When he does move the scene of his fiction beyond the Russian frontier, be it to Frankfurt or the Isle of Wight, it is always to a place visited by the author. He makes some interesting revelations about the role of observation in his creation of character in his study 'On Fathers and Children'. He writes: 'I must confess I never attempted to 'create a character' unless I had for my starting point not an idea, but a living person. Not possessing a great amount of free inventive powers, I always felt the need of some firm ground on which I could plant my feet.'[113] And later of *Virgin Soil*, which received many adverse reviews, he said: 'of the twelve characters . . . two were not studied by me carefully enough on the spot . . . and I do not wish to *invent* in that particular sense. . . . Thus one must gather material.'[114]

No study of the literary aesthetic of Flaubert and Turgenev would be complete without some mention of their concept of 'Beauty' and 'the beautiful'. In his correspondence, Flaubert was prolific in his utterances on this subject. It figures at the very centre of his views on art, and constitutes the essence of what he personally hoped to achieve. As he wrote to George Sand: 'I am seeking above all for *beauty*.'[115] He admired the art of the classical world precisely because of its achievements in this respect: 'What an artist one would be if one had never read anything but beautiful things . . . the Greeks had all that.'[116] He found, on the contrary, writing about life in the bourgeois society of nineteenth-century France diametrically opposed to his concept of beauty. He lamented to Louis Bouilhet in 1853: 'I can't wait to finish the *Bovary* . . . so as to be able to give myself up to pure Beauty.'[117] And of course achievement of this dimension in the domain of form and style was his constant goal, whatever the nature of the subject matter; such achievement was for Flaubert intrinsic to the very nature of artistic creation. 'The moral of Art lies in its very beauty, and I esteem style above all else, Truth comes afterwards.'[118]

Turgenev also believed in the essential link between art and beauty; as his character Bersyenev advises Shubin the young sculptor in *On the Eve*: 'If you don't respond to beauty, if you don't love her wherever you meet her, beauty will elude you in your art.'[119] His views on the power and immortality of beauty are encapsulated in a letter to Pauline Viardot:

> You ask me in what Beauty resides. If despite the ravages of time which destroy the form in which it manifests itself, it still remains. . . . It is that Beauty is the only thing that is immortal, and as long as there remains a trace of its material manifestation, its immortality is assured. Beauty extends over everything, even over death.[120]

Turgenev also seems to have found personal consolation in the ideal of beauty for the sadness and resignation of his life. In the early 1860s, one of the blackest periods of his life, following the change in his relationship with Mme Viardot, he was none the less able to write to the Countess Lambert: 'I feel like a creature who died long ago, who belongs to the past . . . but a creature who has retained a living love for the Good and for the Beautiful.'[121]

Thus Turgenev and Flaubert sought to convey a dimension of truth and beauty in their work, thus raising their art above the level of the mundaneness of the real world, and of their own subject matter. Their essential reproach to Emile Zola was his deliberate refusal to do just that. Flaubert would most certainly have concurred in the sentiments expressed in a phrase from *Faust* that Turgenev frequently quoted as a kind of maxim: 'die Wirklichkeit zum schönen Schein erheben'.[122] Their literary aesthetic reveals a remarkable degree of intellectual kinship, so that even where their tastes vary on the level of detail, their judgements in artistic matters are always guided by the same principles.

Although the question of influence is a vexed one and difficult ever to quantify or prove, there was a certain 'sharing' of literary projects between Flaubert and Turgenev in the 1870s. But this was of necessity a rather one-way process, that is to say that Turgenev was involved to some extent with all of Flaubert's works from *Sentimental Education* onwards. But the latter having no knowledge of either the Russian language or the Russian scene, his encouragement to Turgenev could be only of a very general nature. Flaubert seems to have had an almost physical need to talk about his work, to read out to others the parts already written; typical is his comment to his Russian friend: 'I *need* to explain to you in great detail a plan for a book.' There is good reason to believe that the collaborative discussions between the two writers were not just mutual flattery sessions. Flaubert admits frequently to being struck by the perceptiveness of Turgenev's criticisms; for example, Turgenev thought *Sentimental Education* was a bad choice for a title, and he didn't hesitate to say so.

As far as Turgenev's works are concerned, the sharing was much more a post-publication affair. As soon as his novels and stories came out in French translation, he sent copies to Flaubert who would record his detailed reactions in a letter, often written the minute he had finished reading the volume in question. Thus we have a precise record of his opinion of a good many of Turgenev's works. He also wrote to others of the pleasure he gained from reading the books of 'the good Muscovite'. In the late spring of 1873, *The Torrents of Spring* and *Strange Stories* were published in France; as usual Turgenev sent copies to Flaubert, and as usual the latter was enormously impressed with his friend's literary skill. He commented on these works in a number of letters to other writers. Asking George Sand if she had read *The Unfortunate Girl* he described it as 'simply sublime'. He recommended the same story to Guy de Maupassant and the Princess Mathilde as 'a rare masterpiece'. And on receipt of *The Torrents of Spring* he told his niece Caroline that the book had given him 'a delicious day' and added 'What a man!'[123]

The letters reveal which aspects of Turgenev's work appealed especially to Flaubert. The first work for which he records a reaction is *Scènes de la vie russe* in Louis Viardot's translation. Here it is the suggestive power of the writing that he especially admires: 'one sees and one dreams'. And precisely this ability to provoke an imaginative participation on the part of the reader was, for Flaubert, one of the essentials of artistic achievement. He commented to Louise Colet as early as 1853: 'What seems to me the highest thing in Art . . . (and the most difficult) . . . is to be like nature, that is to make people dream.'[124] He was also moved by the elegiac tone of Turgenev's works, finding in them a 'bitter–sweet perfume, a delightful sadness' that had a profound effect on him.

The value of generalisation in art was a subject pronounced on frequently by Flaubert in his correspondence. In the novel, which he described as 'the scientific form of life' the author 'should proceed by generalities and be more logical than the fortuitous nature of things'.[125] For him, great geniuses were characterised by their ability to incorporate generalisation into their creations, thus making an amalgam of various human types and contributing 'new characters' to the human race. This was another quality of Turgenev that he admired; he told him: 'You manage to encompass general points while writing about the specific.' And of course it was exactly this effect that Flaubert himself hoped to achieve in *Madame Bovary*. Of the *general* application and relevance of this work he asserted confidently: 'My poor Bovary is doubtless suffering and weeping in twenty French villages at this very moment.'[126]

Flaubert, who always went to such pains over the psychology of his own female characters, Emma and Salammbô especially, was also very impressed by Turgenev's portrayal of women. The characterisation of Elena (in *On the Eve*) and Zinochka (in *First Love*) prompted him to write: 'The creation of women is one of your strong points. They are both ideal and real. They have the attraction of saintliness' (letter to Turgenev, at the end of March 1863). He admired, too, the psychology of the handling of the love story in these two works.

The very number of instances of coincidence of view and convergence of experience on the part of Flaubert and Turgenev must surely make them something of a special case in the field of comparative literature. The points of contact which contributed to the affinity between the minds of these two great men were listed precisely and accurately by Guy de Maupassant. We leave this question of the close intellectual relationship between Flaubert and Turgenev with the conclusion of this mutual friend:

These two men love each other in a fraternal friendship: they love each other through the sympathy of genius, through their universal knowledge and shared habits of thought. . . . Affinities of talent, philosophy and mind, similarities in taste, life and dreams, a convergence of literary tendencies, in exalted ideals, in admiration and in erudition established between them so many points of perpetual contact.[127]

Textual note on the letters

Eighty-nine of the manuscripts of Turgenev's letters to Flaubert are in the Collection Spoelberch de Lovenjoul at the Bibliothèque de l'Institut de France, Chantilly. Forty-eight of Flaubert's replies are housed in the Département des Manuscrits at the Bibliothèque Nationale, Paris. There is one other at the Bibliothèque Municipale, Rouen. These have been consulted in the preparation of this edition and, as a result, it has been possible to make a number of corrections and changes to the texts as previously published. For those letters remaining inaccessible in manuscript, a concordance has been established between the texts of Halpérine-Kaminsky (*Ivan Tourguéneff d'après sa correspondance avec ses amis français*) and the Soviet Academy edition of Turgenev's correspondence; and in the case of Flaubert, the Gérard-Gailly (*Lettres inédites à Tourguéneff*), the Conard and the Club de l'honnête homme editions of the complete correspondence.[1] None of Flaubert's letters to Turgenev has yet appeared in the Pléiade edition.

I have resisted the temptation to standardise the texts of Flaubert and Turgenev, preferring to respect inconsistencies in matters such as the underlining or use of inverted commas for the titles of works. This is significant, for St Julian, St Anthony, Bouvard and Pécuchet, etc. are often discussed as if they were real people rather than works of fiction.

Both writers are idiosyncratic in their use of punctuation. Flaubert uses commas very sparingly; I have tried to reflect his usage wherever possible in an English context. Turgenev uses dashes with great eccentricity in French; many have been omitted or replaced with commas, but some have been retained as indicators of a quirk of style.

Turgenev usually dates his letters clearly; Flaubert rarely puts a full date on his, but it is often possible to supplement through cross-referring to that of his correspondent; thus it has been possible to date more accurately some letters.

All letters are dated according to the Gregorian calendar. The Russian calendar was twelve days behind in the nineteenth century. When writing to Flaubert from Russia, Turgenev himself gave the western European date only.

Transliterations of Russian names and words are in accordance with British Standard no.2979 (1958).

Flaubert's pet name for Turgenev was 'le Moscove', the Muscovite, to which he frequently attached adjectives such as 'the good', 'the dear', 'the gigantic' and which he invariably used with close friends when referring to Turgenev. The latter rather took exception to this name, however, not in fact being a Muscovite, so Flaubert refrained from using it as a direct form of address in his letters to him.

I acknowledge a debt of gratitude to M. Jacques Suffel, Conservateur-adjoint at the Bibliothèque Spoelberch de Lovenjoul, Chantilly.

I
March 1863–April 1872

Flaubert and Turgenev met on 28 February 1863 at Magny's restaurant in Paris. In his account of this latest in a series of literary
dinners, the diarist Edmond de Goncourt seems delighted with the
Russian newcomer, describing him as 'an author of delicate talent' and
physically as 'a charming colossus, a gentle giant . . . handsome . . .
modest'.[1] Flaubert joined in the welcoming ovation and Turgenev
proceeded to report to the assembled company on the state of Russian
literature, by now, according to him, fully committed to realism.

The first letter to be exchanged between the two novelists was
written by Turgenev the following day. After this first friendly
contact which runs to five letters, there was a gap in the correspondence, but the relationship was by no means broken off. Turgenev, for
example, spent most of 1866 in Baden Baden working on his novel
Smoke, making only a brief visit to Paris in May, but he must have
been in contact with Flaubert again at this time, as he wrote to Mme
Viardot on the 29th of that month: 'Flaubert has recently left Paris. He
intends to come and spend a few days in Baden.'[2] But of course
Flaubert, the notorious stay-at-home never made the journey. None
the less an indication of the closeness between the two novelists, even
at this early stage, emerges from a letter to Flaubert's niece of the
winter of 1868: 'On Thursday I shall probably dine with my darling
Turgenev.'[3]

Flaubert, during this time, was working on his novel *Sentimental
Education* which was published in 1869. Turgenev made his first visit
to Flaubert's house at Croisset in November 1868, and listened to
readings from the manuscript.

The correspondence between the two was to be further interrupted
by the Franco-Prussian War which broke out on 19 July 1870.
Turgenev, who was in Baden at the time, remained there until the
November. He then joined his friends the Viardots, who had been
financially ruined by the war, in voluntary exile in London. When the
exchange of letters between him and Flaubert resumed in the late
sprint of 1871, both writers express rather dazed reactions to the recent
events in Paris: the end of hostilities with Prussia had been followed by

a popular insurrection and the declaration of the Commune.

During these troubled times, Turgenev made no contribution to the novel form, producing no full-length work between the publication of *Smoke* in 1867, and beginning to work on *Virgin Soil* in 1872. He did, however, write a number of quite remarkable short stories, notably *A Strange Story, Knock . . . Knock . . . Knock . . .* and *King Lear of the Steppe*, all of which were to arouse Flaubert's admiration.

After the disappointing reception of *Sentimental Education*, Flaubert also abandoned the novel for a while, devoting his energies to a dramatic rendering of the Temptation of Saint Anthony, of which subject he had already produced two versions some twenty years previously.

210 rue de Rivoli [Paris]
Sunday [1 March 1863]

Dear Sir,

Allow me to make you a gift of the two enclosed volumes;[4] I shall send you two others[5] to your address near Rouen shortly – for I do not wish to take advantage of your good nature. It would be most kind if you were to come and spend part of tomorrow evening (Monday) at my rooms (210 rue de Rivoli). There will be a few friends, including Mme Viardot who wishes to make your acquaintance. It would be some compensation for the regret I feel at not having met you sooner.

In the meantime,

Yours sincerely,
I. Turgenev

Croisset near Rouen
16 March [1863]

Dear Mr Turgenev,

How grateful I am for the gift you sent me! I have just read your two volumes, and really must tell you that I am delighted with them.

I have considered you a master for a long time. But the more I study you, the more your skill leaves me gaping. I admire the vehement yet restrained quality of your writing, the fellow feeling that extends to the lowest of human creatures and brings landscapes to life. One perceives and one dreams.

Just as when I read *Don Quixote* I feel like going on horseback along a white and dusty road, like eating olives and raw onions in the shade of a cliff face, your *Scenes from Russian Life* make me want to be shaken alone in a telega through snow-covered fields, to the sound of wolves howling. Your work has a bitter–sweet flavour, a sadness that is delightful and penetrates to the very depths of my soul.

What an artist! What a mixture of emotion, irony, observation and colour! And how it is all blended together! How you achieve your effects! What mastery!

You manage to encompass general points while writing about the specific. How many things that I have felt and experienced myself have I found in your work! In *Three Encounters* amongst others, and especially in *Jacob Pasynkov*, in the *Diary of a Superfluous Man*, etc., everywhere.

But what has not received enough praise in your work is the heart, that is, a sustained emotion, an indefinable deep and secret sensibility.

I was very happy to meet you two weeks ago, to shake you by the hand. I renew this gesture, dear colleague, more cordially than ever.

With my very best wishes,

Gustave Flaubert

210 rue de Rivoli Paris
19 March 1863

Dear Mr Flaubert,

Your letter made me blush quite as much as it delighted me – and that's saying a lot. Such praise makes one proud – and I wish I had deserved it. Nevertheless, I am very pleased to have found favour with you and I thank you for saying as much.

I am sending you a book of mine that has just come out.[6] I have another one being published that I will send you as soon as it is finished.[7] You see I spare you nothing now.

Do you not think of coming to Paris before the summer? I should be so happy to continue our relationship that has had such favourable beginnings and which – I can confidently say for my own part – wishes for nothing more than to develop into the most open-hearted friendship.

I shake your hand with all the friendly feelings I already have for you.

With affectionate greetings,

I. Turgenev

Croisset
Tuesday evening [end of March 1863]

My dear colleague,
Your letter was most kind and you are too modest. For I have just read your latest book. I found your essential qualities in it, and more intense, more rarified than ever.

What I admire above all is the distinguished quality of your art – a wonderful thing. You manage to ring true yet avoid banality, to be sentimental without morbidity, and comic without being at all low. Without looking for high drama, you achieve it none the less by the sheer professionalism of your tragic effects. You seem very casual, but you have great skill, 'the skin of the fox combined with that of the lion', as Montaigne said.

Elena's is a fine story.[8] I like this character, as well as Shubin and all the others. While reading you one says to oneself 'I've experienced that'. Thus I believe that page 51 will be felt with greater intensity by no one than by me. What a psychologist! But I'd need many lines to express all my thoughts on that.

As for your *First Love*, I understand it all the better for its being the story of one of my closest friends. All old romantics (and I who slept with a dagger under my pillow am one) should be grateful to you for this little story that has so much to say about their youth! What a real live girl Zinochka is. The creation of women is one of your strong points. They are both ideal and real. They have the attraction of saintliness. But what dominates this work, indeed the whole collection, is the two lines: 'I had no bad feelings towards my father. On the contrary he had, so to speak, increased in stature in my eyes.' That strikes me as being startlingly profound. Will people pick it up? I don't know. But for me, it is sublime.

Yes, dear colleague, I hope that our relationship will not stand still, and that our mutual sympathy will turn into friendship.

In the meantime, one thousand handshakes from your
Gustave Flaubert

210 rue de Rivoli Paris
18 April 1863

My dear colleague,
I don't need, I hope, to tell you how much pleasure your second letter gave me – and more than pleasure! If I didn't reply straight-away, it was because I had to extricate myself from a host of

disagreeable little matters that made me ill-humoured and lazy at the same time. These miseries continue, but my conscience will not permit me to delay any longer. I have been counting on, and still do, on your indulgence – and above all I want to thank you and shake you by the hand.

I am very glad to have your approval and you should be convinced of it: I well know that an artist and man of good will such as yourself reads a host of things between the lines of a book, for which he generously appreciates the author's effort: but it doesn't make any difference. Praise coming from you is worth gold – and I pocket it with pride and gratitude.

Shall we not see each other during the summer? An hour of good, frank conversation is worth a hundred letters. I'm leaving Paris in a week's time to go and settle in Baden. Will you not come there? There are trees there such as I've seen nowhere else – and right on the tops of the mountains. The atmosphere is young and vigorous and it's poetic and gracious at the same time. It does a power of good to your eyes and to your soul. When you sit at the foot of one of these giants, it seems as if you take in some of its sap – and it's good and beneficial. Really, come to Baden, even if it were only for a few days. You will take away with you some wonderful colours for your palette.

Before I leave, you will receive a book by me which has just been published.[9] I am cramming you full – but you are partly to blame.

A thousand friendly greetings, keep well, work well, and come to Baden.

Yours

I. Turgenev

Croisset near Rouen
20 March[10] [20 April 1863]

Cram me full then, dear colleague! I await your book impatiently and I shall read it with delight, I am sure.

I also have had a number of little aggravations just lately. The affinity between us is complete, you see.

I don't think I shall be able to go to Baden, because I shall have several obligations that will disturb my routine this summer. When will you be back? And send me your address.

I shall spend the whole of June or the whole of August in Paris. In any case, we shall see each other next winter.

A thousand very long and very vigorous handshakes from your

Gustave Flaubert

[Paris]
Saturday morning [May 1866][11]

My dear great Turgenev,
Be ready, for next Friday, to dine at the house of a beautiful lady friend of mine, where you will find yourself amongst people who admire you: Théophile Gautier, Renan, de Goncourt etc.[12]
I'm still counting on a little visit from you tomorrow, at about 4 o'clock.

Yours
G. Flaubert

3 Thiergartenstrasse Baden
26 May 1868

My dear friend,
I'm very grateful to you for thinking of writing to me. Your letter gave me much pleasure – for it re-established relations between us and because it showed that you liked my book.[13]
These days every single artist has something of the critic in him. The artist is very great in you – and you know how much I love and admire it; but I also have a high opinion of the critic and I am very happy to have his approval. I well know that your friendship for me counts for something in all this: but I have the feeling that a master has stood in front of my picture, has looked at it and has nodded his head with an air of satisfaction. Well, I'll say again that this has given me great pleasure.
I was very sorry not to have seen you in Paris – I only stayed there three days, and I regret even more that you are not coming to Baden this year. Your novel has you in harness[14] – that's good – I await it with the greatest impatience – but could you not take a few days rest, to the profit of your friends here? Since the first time I saw you (you know, in a sort of inn on the other bank of the Seine) I have felt a great liking for you – there are few men, particularly French men, with whom I feel so relaxed and at ease and yet at the same time so stimulated. It seems to me that I could talk to you for weeks on end, but then we are a pair of moles burrowing away in the same direction.
All this means that I should be very glad to see you. I'm leaving for Russia in a fortnight's time, but I shan't stay there long, and I shall be back by the end of July – and I shall go to Paris to see my daughter[15] who will probably have made me a grandfather by then. I shall be game enough to come and chase after you even at home – if you are there. Or will you come to Paris? But I must see you.

In the meantime I wish you good fortune. The living, human truth that you pursue indefatigably can only be captured on good days. You have had some – you will have more – and many of them.

Keep well; I also embrace you – and with true friendship.

I. Turgenev

42 boulevard du Temple Paris
25 July [1868]

My dear Turgenev,

This is simply to remind you of your promise. You were supposed to be in Paris at the end of July or the beginning of August. As for me, I am here, and I await you.

So as to avoid your making unnecessary arrangements, here is my programme: from 30 July (next Thursday) until 8 August I shall be at Saint-Gratien at the Princess Mathilde's.[16] Then I shall return to Paris for two days. I shall then spend another two days at Dieppe at one of my nieces. Then I shall return to Croisset, to get on with my book.

We *must* spend a few good hours together.

I embrace you wishing you cooler weather than we're having in Paris, and I remain yours

G. Flaubert

3 Thiergartenstrasse Baden
Tuesday, 28 July 1868

My dear friend,

It was very kind of you to have thought of me, and to have given me, as you say, your programme. I have been here for 4 days – but unfortunately I did not return from Russia alone: I brought a fine attack of gout with me – it took hold of me in Moscow and I have had a relapse since my arrival in Baden. Here I am on a chaise longue with all the attendant miseries – 'oil of horsechestnut' etc., etc.

However it is less violent than last year and I have not lost hope of making my journey to France towards the middle of next month – and then, according to the *programme*, I shall hunt you out in your *den*. I admit I am quite curious to see it.

I haven't seen Du Camp,[17] who is supposed to be here: I have not left my room since I arrived here. In two or three days' time I shall perhaps be able to do my errands by carriage.

Keep well and work with voracity and tranquillity – it's the best way. I give you a friendly embrace.

> Your
> I. Turgenev

> 3 Thiergartenstrasse Baden
> Tuesday, 18 August '68

My dear friend,
  I have waited until now to reply to your kind little note, because I was still hoping to be able to announce my arrival; but my devilish gout is obstinately refusing to leave me, and I cannot yet contemplate any kind of long journey. It's annoying – but what can I do about it? I shall come as soon as I can; and in the meantime I embrace you and beg you to present my respects to your mother, whom I shall be very happy to meet.

> Work hard in the meantime.
> I. Turgenev

> Croisset
> Sunday evening [23 August 1868]

I am cross at the delay, my dear Turgenev, firstly because I want to see you, and then because I know you are ill. Look after yourself! Get better! Gout comes in sporadic attacks, I think? So when your attack is over, write 'I'm coming' and come. I shall not shift from home for a long time yet. You are sure to find me here.
  I shake both your hands very vigorously.

> G. Flaubert

> Croisset
> Wednesday [18 November 1868]

Ah! At last! We are going to see each other, dear friend!
  I advise you to take the 8 a.m. express train, which arrives in Rouen at 10.40 a.m. Once at Rouen you will find a carriage which will bring you to Croisset in twenty minutes.
  But what would be even better would be to write back to me straightaway telling me the time of your arrival. And I will meet you. Because I have a burning desire to see you and to embrace you.

So, until Sunday. I'm counting on you without fail. But a line in answer between now and then, please though.

Yours more than ever

G. Flaubert

Hotel Byron rue Lafitte [Paris]
Thursday [19 November 1868]

I shall leave on Sunday, my dear friend, at 8 o'clock in the morning by the express train, and I shall be very happy to see you straightaway at the station.

Until Sunday then, and a thousand friendly greetings.

I. Turgenev

Hotel Byron rue Lafitte [Paris]
Tuesday, 24 November '68

My dear friend,

The cheese has just arrived; I shall take it to Baden with me, and with every mouthful we shall think of Croisset and of the delightful day I spent there. Decidedly I feel that there is a real affinity between the two of *us*.

If all of your novel is as good as the extracts you read to me, you will have written a masterpiece, I'm telling you.

I don't know if you've read the book I'm sending you; in any case, put it on one of the shelves of your library.[18]

Present my respects to your mother – and let me embrace you.

Your

I. Turgenev

P.S.   My address is: Carlsruhe, poste restante. It would be very kind if you were to send me a photograph of yourself. Here is one of me that looks very forbidding.

P.P.S.   Find another title. 'Sentimental Education' is wrong.

Hotel Prince Max Carlsruhe
Monday, 25 January '69

But I must have news of you, my dear friend. Let's see now – in two words: where are you – and how is the novel going? I am writing to you at Croisset, and perhaps you are in Paris, sniffing out what's new.

In any case, I don't think you'll stay there long.

I have not yet thanked you for the photograph, which makes you look very military and well groomed – but it's you all right – and it's always good to look at it. Why don't you have some good ones taken?

I have often thought of Croisset, and I think to myself that it's a fine nest to fledge songbirds in. As for me, I have done almost nothing. I have embarked on a task that I find repugnant and I am floundering about sadly in it. There's no going back, but when it's finished, I shall give a great sigh of relief! It's a sort of anthology of literary reminiscences that I promised my publisher; I have never worked in that field – and it's not at all amusing. Oh! Two hours of being Sainte-Beuve![19] I'd like to know if he enjoys it very much.

My best greetings to your honourable mother, who seems to me the best possible of mamas one could imagine, and a good vigorous handshake to you.

Your
I. Turgenev

P.S.   I am here for the whole winter because my friends the Viardots are here. It's not very gay, Carlsruhe, but it's better than its reputation. I shall come to Paris towards the end of March.

Croisset
2 February [1869]

My dear friend,

I am still at Croisset, that is to say I came back here yesterday, having spent all of last week in Paris, in search of the most ridiculous information imaginable: funerals, cemeteries and undertakers on the one hand, seizure of goods and court procedures on the other etc., etc.[20] In short I am crushed with fatigue and boredom. My interminable novel is making me sick and weighing me down, and I've got at least another four months to go.

I'm burning with impatience to see your literary criticism, because yours will be that of a practitioner – an important point. What shocks me in my friends Sainte-Beuve and Taine,[21] is that they don't take sufficient account of *Art*, of the work itself, of its construction, of its style, in short of everything that constitutes Beauty. In La Harpe's[22] day, everyone was a grammarian, nowadays they are all historians, that's the only difference. With your way of feeling that's so original and so intense, your criticism will be the equal of your creative work, I'm sure.

And I also think very often about the afternoon you spent at my old homestead. You charmed everybody here, my mother and my niece often speak of you and enquire after you.

As for me, you know how much affection I have felt for you since the day we met. Why do we not live in the same country?

I shall be in Paris towards Easter. Don't come before.

I embrace you very heartily.

G. Flaubert

Croisset
Wednesday, 17 March [1869]

My dear friend,

I remind you of your promise, that is to say, I'm counting on seeing you in Paris in the week after Easter.

I count on arriving there the day before Easter. What about you? Drop me a line as soon as you receive this.

I embrace you as I love you, that is with all my heart.

G. Flaubert

Hotel Prince Max Carlsruhe
Sunday, 21 March 1869

My dear friend,

Your letter addressed to 'Stuttgart or Baden' has only just reached me here. I hasten to say that I'm leaving here for Paris on *Wednesday*, and that I arrive there on *Thursday* at 5 o'clock in the morning. I'm staying at the Hotel Byron, rue Lafitte. I'm spending a week in Paris. There is no need to say how pleased I shall be to see you. In the meantime I embrace you with all my friendship.

I. Turgenev

P.S.   Remember me to your mother.

Croisset
Thursday morning [25 March 1869]

If you have nothing better to do on Sunday afternoon, come and see me at my place at 42 boulevard du Temple.

I shall arrive in Paris on Saturday evening. My plan is to dine with the Hussons.[23] In any case, save Tuesday for me.

I'm delighted at the idea of seeing you again soon. In the meantime I embrace you.

                                        G. Flaubert

Drop me a line at boulevard du Temple to let me know your programme for the week. I'll fit in with it. How I'm dying to have a good chat with you!

                                Hotel Byron rue Lafitte Paris
                                    Friday [26 March 1869]

Dear friend,
    I shall come and see you on Sunday at 2 o'clock; is that all right? We must do all sorts of things together.
                            Yours
                                    I. Turgenev

                            Hotel Byron rue Lafitte [Paris]
                                Saturday [27 March 1869]

Dear friend,
    I wrote to you yesterday that I would come and see you on Sunday at 2 o'clock; but I shan't be able to come until 3 *on the dot*.
                            Yours
                                    I. Turgenev

                                    Thursday [Autumn 1869]

I thought I was going to get some *real* news from my old Turgenev, that is to say a gigantic epistle, to compensate for his silence of nearly six months' duration. But no! He has forgotten me, it is unkind.
    For my part, I have nothing to say to him. My life is less and less gay. It is even dreadfully sad, and I am working like umpteen million negroes.
    Notwithstanding, I embrace the said old fellow tenderly.
                            His
                                G. Flaubert

3 Thiergartenstrasse Baden
Sunday, 30 January 1870

My dear friend,
    In the first number of a Russian magazine published in St Peters-
burg, and which is called the 'Russian Messenger' (it is as you might
say the Russian 'Revue des 2 Mondes'),[24] there is a huge article on your
book[25] (it's only the first part). It is analysed in detail and the whole
subject explained – both the author and his work are highly praised;
this article is entitled 'The New French Society'. I'm telling you all this
because it may be of interest, although you are hammering away at
something else at the moment.
    I'm leaving Baden in 4 or 5 days' time – I'm going to spend two
months in Weimar (my address is: Hotel de Russie, Weimar, Grand
Duchy of Saxe-Weimar) and I shall pass through Paris before returning to Russia in April.
    Let me have news of you. Are you working hard? Your 'Anthony'
often crosses my mind. Last night in bed I reread the scene of the 'Club
de l'Intelligence' and the Spaniard made me laugh out loud.[26]
    Give my regards to Mme Sand, to Du Camp and all the rest, I shake
your hand with all the strength of my friendship.
                                                    I. Turgenev

4 rue Murillo Parc Monceau [Paris]
14 February [1870]

My dear friend,
    It is very kind of you to point out to me a review where my
unfortunate book receives praise! For things have not been a bed of
roses on that front. You had also mentioned a Berlin magazine to me?
I'd like to know the title. All this for Lévy of course.[27]
    I find (and I make no secret of it) that I've been treated unfairly.
There is nothing more ridiculous than making out that one is mis-
understood. Nevertheless it's what I think. *Habent sua fata libelli,*[28] as
Horace said – and Prudhomme.
    My studies on the good Mr Anthony (on whose account you were
anxious) have been suspended for two weeks, spent exclusively in
organising a performance at the Odéon, for the monument to
Bouilhet.[29] I am chairman of the Subscription Committee, and I've
had to do everything myself in order to raise as much money as
possible. For two weeks, and in spite of bad attack of 'flu, I was
making calls all over Paris, spending seven hours a day in a carriage!

What a strain on the nerves! All went well, thank goodness, and it's all over!

Someone at the Gaiety Theatre has asked me for my fairy piece *Le Château des coeurs*. I shall read it as soon as my larynx has cleared itself. And what about you, dear and great friend, what are you up to? What are you dreaming up? What are you writing? When you return to Paris, make sure you stay longer!

The moments spent with you recently have been the only good times I've had in the last eight months! You can't imagine how isolated I feel on the intellectual front! That's why I seize upon you so avidly, as soon as you turn up.

My noble motherland is becoming more and more idiotic. The general stupidity is having an effect on individuals. Gradually each one sides with all the rest.

You seem to me to be a happy man – and I should be jealous of you if I didn't love you dearly.

I embrace you.

> Your
> Gustave Flaubert

> Hotel de Russie Weimar
> 20 February '70

My dear friend,

Mr Julian Schmidt's article on 'Sentimental Education' has not yet appeared in the 'Preussische Jahrbücher'; as soon as it comes out, I'll send it to you. If you would like, I'll ask him to send you his article on 'Mme Bovary'. It came out last year. The second issue of 'The European Messenger' (Russian) that I have just received contains the second and final part of the article I told you about – and it's more or less a very detailed summary of the novel. The general opinion is that *woman* plays too large a part in the life of Frédéric – and the question is asked whether all young French men are like that.

Yes, people have certainly been unfair to you, but this is the time to brace yourself and hurl a masterpiece at the reading public. Your 'Anthony' could be such a projectile. Don't tarry too long over it, that's my refrain. Don't forget that people judge you according to the standards that you yourself have established, and you're bearing the weight of your past. You have energy; 'el hombre debe ser feroz'[30] as the Spanish proverb says – and artists especially. Even if your book has only gripped a dozen people of any worth – then that is enough. You understand I'm saying all this not to console you, but to spur you on.

I have been here for about ten days – and my sole preoccupation is keeping warm. The houses are badly built here, and the iron stoves are useless. You'll see a very little thing by me in the March edition of the 'Revue des 2 Mondes'.[31] It's nothing very much. I'm working on something more '*solid*', that is, I'm getting ready to work.

I shall go to Paris before returning to Russia; that will be towards the end of April. I shall stay a good ten days – we shall see each other often.

If you see Mme Sand, give her my regards. Greetings to Du Camp and the Husson family.

I embrace you and wish you courage! You are Flaubert after all.

Your
I.T.

[Paris]
Saturday evening [April 1870]

I was very sorry to hear in your last letter that we shan't see each other this summer, my dear friend. I had counted on a good chance to let myself go with you, before your departure for Russia. But how difficult everything in this life is!

The great sadness I've had this winter has been the death of my closest friend after Bouilhet, a good lad called Jules Duplan[32] who was devoted to me. These two deaths, coming one on top of the other, have overwhelmed me. Add to that the pitiful state of two other friends (not such close friends, it's true, but none the less they were part of my immediate circle). I'm referring to Feydeau's[33] paralysis and the *madness* (*sic*) of Jules de Goncourt. The loss of Sainte-Beuve, money worries, my novel's lack of success etc., etc. even down to my manservant's rheumatism (the one who looks like Lassouche[34]), everything, as you can see, has conspired to aggravate me. And to do so to no mean extent.

I can easily say that the only good thing to happen to me for a long time was your last visit, which was too short. Why do we live so far away from one another? You are (I think) the only man I enjoy talking to. I can't see that anybody else bothers about art and poetry! The plebiscite,[35] socialism, the International and other such garbage are cluttering up everybody's brains.

I fear I shan't be able to accept your invitation this summer. Here's why. In four or five days' time I shall return to Croisset, where I'm going to write the preface to the volume of Bouilhet's verse straight-away. It will take me two or three months – after which, I shall tackle *St Anthony* which will be interrupted in October by the rehearsals for *Aïssé*.[36] They will rob me of a good two months. So between now and next New Year I shall have barely six weeks to devote to the good hermit. I would like to spend not more than two years on that fellow. So you see how pressed for time I am. I must get on with that work, as quickly as possible, as I'm already starting to feel I've had enough of it. I have consumed too many books, one on top of the other – but it was in order to make myself numb to my personal sorrows.

Send me your news when you're at home in Russia – and think of me often, because I often think of you, and I embrace you, *ex imo*

G. Flaubert

My mother was, as they say, very *touched* by your kind regards.

Croisset nr Rouen
1 May 1871

I have just heard of the misfortune that has struck you, my dear friend, and my first thought was for you.[37] I like you too much to try and write commonplaces. But I am very sad and I embrace you.

What a year! What a year! Where are you? What will become of you? Where will you live now? What are your plans? Let me have news of you if you have the strength and if this piece of paper reaches you. For you know I love you and I remain yours

G. Flaubert

16 Beaumont Street Marylebone London
6 May 1871

Fortunately, my dear friend, fortunately the news was completely false! Mme V. whom I see every day is no more dead than she is fifty-four years old. If the news had been true, I don't think I should have been able to write back to you . . . I can tell you now that your letter moved me deeply. It's a very fine thing to feel that one has a true friend – and I thank you for offering me proof of such a feeling.

I have been here for three weeks – I spent the end of the winter and the beginning of spring in Russia – I am staying here until 1 August. I shall stop in Paris – if there is still a Paris then – and I hope to see you. Perhaps you will come to Baden, where we shall live for a while like moles hiding in their holes, and you could hide there with us. But let me have your news before then. Did you ever get the letter I wrote to you at the beginning of the year? What have you been doing during all this awful storm? Did you stay at Croisset the whole time? Did you manage, in spite of all your efforts at solitude and concentration, did you manage to avoid being shaken up like those wisps of straw that whirl about alarmingly and in futile sadness in open barn doorways? Have you been working – or was the effort of living life – heavy and empty – from day to day enough? I am not French, and yet I've done hardly anything but that. Oh we have hard times to live through, those of us who are *born spectators*. What is Anthony doing? He has become lodged in my mind.

I am in England – not for the pleasure of being here – but because my friends, who have been just about ruined by this war, have come here to try to earn a little money. The English have some good qualities – but they all – even the most intelligent – lead a very hard life. It takes some getting used to – like their climate. But then where else can one go?

What is Madame Flaubert doing? Remember me to her. Have you heard from Du Camp? He has disappeared in the confusion, like so many others.

Write me a note. Again thank you for the affection you bear me. I embrace you with all the strength of my own.

Your friend
I. Turgenev

P.S.   There is no point in saying that I didn't receive your letter until today.

16 Beaumont Street Marylebone London
13 June 1871

My dear friend,

If I didn't answer you sooner, it's because I didn't have the courage. These events in Paris[38] have left me stupefied. I kept silent as one does in a railway carriage when entering a tunnel: the infernal noise overwhelms one and makes one's head spin. Now that it is more or less over, I'm confirming that *most certainly* I shall come and see you and hear 'Anthony' in August. It will be between the 15th and the 20th. I have been invited to shoot grouse in Scotland at the beginning of August, but I shall be free on the 15th and on the way back to Baden I'll stop in Paris or in Rouen – I mean at Croisset – if you are there. I'm very pleased to hear that you are half way with your book; you risk nothing in hurrying it up a bit: on the contrary. I shall listen with my ears, eyes and brain wide open – I'm almost certain that it will be very fine.

I won't summon you to Germany any more; I understand your reluctance to set foot there. Nor do I want to say everything that has been going through my mind on the subject of France: it would all have to be summed up in a few words – and that's impossible for me; when we see each other, we will decide the question at length and taking all our time; the result will be no light matter of course. I don't know if it's Russia who should avenge you as you say; for the moment Germany is very strong – and she will probably remain so as long as we shall live.

Give me news of Du Camp if you have any. I heard that Mme Husson had gone mad and then that she was dead: is it true?

I remember that my swimming instructor (he was also a Prussian) was always shouting 'Keep your mouth out of the water – schwere Noth! As long as you keep your mouth out of the water – you're a man!'

You have remained a man through all this, because you have been able to work: now things will be easier.

Thank Mme Flaubert and your niece for their greetings. As for you, I embrace you – and until I see you in August!

I. Turgenev

Croisset near Rouen
Saturday, 17 June [1871]

It's agreed, my dear friend. With great impatience, I expect you between the 15th and the 20th August. Those dates suite me. Moreover all dates suit me, so long as I can see you.

You must find me rather ridiculous with my hatred of Prussia? It's that especially that makes me angry: it has inspired in me the sentiments of a twelfth-century barbarian. But what to do about it? Do you think that in other ages men of letters, *doctors*, behaved like savages?

I spent the whole of last week in Paris. There is something even more pitiful than the ruins, it's the mentality of the population. People are hovering between cretinism and raging madness. This is no exaggeration.

Ah! I would like to be able to forget about France, my contemporaries and humanity! All of that makes me heave with disgust. I'm saddened to the very depths of my being; and now that I've seen Paris, I find it very hard to work.

Adieu, or rather until we meet. In anticipation of that pleasure. I embrace you.

G. Flaubert

Yes, Mme Husson has gone mad (suicidal monomania)! I haven't seen her, but I've seen Du Camp, who also seemed to me to be 'cracked'. Keep this to yourself of course.

Eighteen months ago, I diagnosed the mental disorder of France from two clear symptoms: (i) the success of *La Lanterne*;[39] (ii) the success of Troppmann.[40]

There is hysteria about the fire of Paris. Not to mention the other factors involved which I think I know about.

4 rue Murillo parc Monceau [Paris]
1 August [1871]

My dear friend,

I'm reminding you of your promise, that is, *I'm counting* on your coming to Croisset between the 15th and 20th of this month. I would appreciate it if you would let me know *which day* to expect you. Until then, I embrace you most heartily.

Your
G. Flaubert

How many things I have to tell you, my dear friend! How pleased I shall be to see you. How I'm dying to read you the first half of *Saint Anthony*.

Arrange things in advance so that you can spend several days with me.

4 rue Murillo parc Monceau Paris
[second week in August 1871]

My dear friend,

I beg your pardon for repeating my question, but I really need to know straightaway when I shall have the pleasure – or rather the happiness – of having you all to myself in my old homestead, because I have quite a lot of business to attend to here in Paris and I don't want to *miss you*: it would be too much of a disappointment.

According to your promise, I expect you at Croisset between the 15th and the 20th of this month. I wish you were there already.

I'll see you soon then, dear friend, and all the best.

G. Flaubert

Towards the 20th rather than the 15th don't you think?

4 rue Murillo parc Monceau Paris
Sunday 13 [August 1871]

My dear friend,
   I know you are supposed to return to London on the 15th.
   I beg you to answer *straightaway* to let me know which day I should expect you at Croisset. Don't change your plans, but don't come without letting me know.
   If I hear nothing, I'll expect you in my old homestead *next Saturday* the 18th. Does that suit you? In any case, I shall leave Paris on Friday morning. If you would like to come on Thursday, give me warning. I'll bring forward my return. And arrange things so as to stay at Croisset for several days. I have a great thirst for your company; in anticipation of our meeting, I embrace you.

G. Flaubert

I suppose you are coming back via Dieppe.

Allean House Pitlochry (Scotland)
14 August 1871

My dear friend, your two notes have caught up with me here – in the depths of Scotland, where I am shooting grouse at a friend's place. I leave here the day after tomorrow, the 16th; I leave London the following day, the 17th and I arrive in Paris on the 18th. I wish you were in Paris that day and that I didn't have to go to Croisset – for my time is horribly short. In Paris I shall be at the Hotel Byron, 20 rue Lafitte. Arrange things so that there is a note from you when I arrive. In order to be doubly sure, I'll write this letter out again and send a copy to Croisset.
   I embrace you and I'll see you soon! Get Anthony ready!

Yours
I. Turgenev

Paris
Wednesday morning 16 [August 1871]

At last a letter from you! But if you hadn't enjoyed yourself so much at the shoot, poor old *Saint Anthony* and his author would have had a bit more of your time.
   I absolutely have to leave Paris this very day. That's why you have to come to Croisset, where I expect you on Saturday. There are

several express trains. But I hope that in spite of all your preoccupations, it won't be like last time and you'll stay only for the afternoon.

Send me a note by telegraph telling me at what time I shall see you at last.

Yours

G. Flaubert

Croisset

Monday evening [21 August 1871]

No, my dear friend, I am not cross with you, but I felt disappointed, because I'd been counting on you, and I forgive you on condition that you will devote *several* days to me in October.

The thought that I shall see you this winter quite at leisure delights me like the promise of an oasis. The comparison is the right one, if only you knew how isolated I am! Who is there to talk to now? Who is there in our wretched country who still 'cares about literature'? Perhaps one single man? Me! The wreckage of a lost world, an old fossil of romanticism! You will revive me, you'll do me good.

My mother thanks you for your kind regards. My niece sends you hers. I embrace you very heartily.

G. Flaubert

Villa Viardot Baden-Baden

18 November 1871

My dear friend,

After all sorts of miseries and delays caused by another attack of gout and business matters that are nearly as bad as the gout, I'm leaving tomorrow for Paris, I arrive on Monday – if nothing befalls me – and I shall see you on Tuesday, as I suppose you'll be there, and I'm sending this letter to the rue Murillo. So I'll see you soon – the day after you get this letter – I embrace you.

Your

I. Turgenev

Paris

[25 November 1871]

My dear friend,

I have been here since *Monday* – but on the *very day* of my arrival I was *seized* with an attack of gout (I hope it's the last) and I'm going out today for the first time, but I couldn't climb your staircase yet. *I'll come tomorrow at 1 o'clock* – and I'll get to you somehow or other. I thought of writing to tell you to come here – but I'm in a house (the Viardots') that's still in a real state of chaos and then I was cross at being in bed. So until tomorrow – I shall be very pleased to see you.

I'm living at 48 rue de Douai – but don't come, I'll come to you.

Your
I. Turgenev

48 rue de Douai
Sunday 10 a.m. [26 November 1871]

My dear friend,

I thought I should be able to come and see you today, but I see now that it would be impossible for me, I'll come tomorrow at *1 o'clock on the dot.*

It's not that life is more difficult – but it's becoming more and more difficult to *undertake* to do anything at all. I'm becoming more and more snowed under by life's events.

Until tomorrow, your old faithful.

I. Turgenev

Paris
Monday 9 a.m. [27 November 1871]

My dear friend,

When I wrote to you that it was difficult to undertake anything at all, I never said a truer word. This last night, the ankle of my bad foot swelled up quite suddenly, and now I can neither put on a boot nor put my foot to the ground. So 'Anthony' will have to be postponed – it's really awful luck – unless you would like to come here yourself with the manuscript or shall we wait a couple of days – this kind of attack rarely lasts more than 48 hours.

Here I am, all sheepish, and I shake your hand in disappointment.

Your old
I. Turgenev

[Paris]
Tuesday 11.30 a.m. [28 November 1871]

My dear friend,

This is what has happened. An uncle of mine, Mr Nicholas

Turgenev, an excellent man, worthy of respect has died recently in Paris, and I have just received a telegramme from Petersburg asking me to write an obituary notice, and it must be sent off by tomorrow evening. I have accepted, and so here I am shackled to the task. So dear old Anthony will have to be good enough to wait until the day after tomorrow – as tomorrow I must take my article to his family who live at Bougival to get certain information etc., etc. So until Thursday!

Your note of today's date was not delivered by your manservant. He probably mistook the house. Number 48 rue de Douai is on the corner of the place Vintimille.

A thousand friendly greetings.

I. Turgenev

48 rue de Douai
Paris Friday, 19 January '72

My gout has let go of me again, my dear friend – I'm sorry about all these stupid misunderstandings, and to have given you so much trouble in vain, but damn it all, the thing must come off. Which day do you want:

Tuesday
Wednesday
or
Saturday

of next week? And if I am not dead (as the 'Times' makes out[41]) I shall have myself carried to your place rather than . . .

Anyway, I await your answer.

Your
I. Turgenev

48 rue de Douai Paris
Monday [12 February 1872]

My dear friend,

I see that your invitation is for Friday, Mme Viardot has her musical evenings on Fridays, which I cannot miss. I simply want to say that I have to be home by a quarter to ten. I hope that won't upset your plans.

A thousand friendly freetings.

Your old
I. Turgenev

Paris
Wednesday morning [14 February 1872]

My dear great man,

I enclose a note from Princess Mathilde asking me (i) if I think you remember her, and (ii) if you would like to dine at her house. I took the liberty of answering yes to both of these questions. What's more, I gave her your address, which she asked for.

As for Friday, nothing's changed. You'll just leave a little earlier, that's all. I'll collect you at six o'clock.

Yours
G. Flaubert

[Paris]
Thursday [late February 1872]

My old Flaubert, I forgot yesterday to warn you not to say anything to or in front of Viardot about my having dined at the princess's;[42] he has a great hatred for the Empire (I'll tell you why one day) and he would be upset to know that I mix with his *enemies*. Does Mme V. know where I've been? You are expected this evening. There will only be me.

Your faithful
I.T.

Croisset
Tuesday [16 April 1872]

I am still too shattered to write to you at length.[43] I simply want to thank you for your kind letter.

When are you leaving Paris? When are you coming back?

I still know nothing of the state of my affairs, and I can make no plans for the future. For the moment I'm staying on at Croisset, which now belongs to my niece (the one you know).

Thank M. Viardot for sending me his book.[44] I shall read it as soon as my head has cleared.

Have a good journey and come back quickly. I'm counting on seeing you in July, as we agreed.

I embrace you very heartily.

Your
G. Flaubert

II

June 1872–September 1875

Flaubert's mother died at Croisset on 6 April 1872 in her seventy-eighth year. The letter in which Turgenev expressed his condolences has not survived. Flaubert's depressed state of mind at this time led to a two-month break in his correspondence with his Russian friend, and that autumn Turgenev was prevented from making his promised visit to Normandy by successive attacks of gout.

However, the two novelists had planned to spend Easter 1873 together in the country at Nohant, George Sand's château. Flaubert arrived as arranged on the Saturday before Easter, although Turgenev had written to say that he might be delayed. Flaubert wrote urging him to come; he eventually arrived on the Wednesday evening; thus the projected week's stay was reduced to two days. Such occurrences were frequent with Turgenev, and a source of great frustration to Flaubert.

That autumn, Turgenev finally made his promised visit to Croisset, staying from 2 to 5 October, an exceptionally long time for this notorious bird of passage. The following month, Patrice Macmahon, a Marshal of France who had distinguished himself in the Crimean War, was elected president of the Third Republic by a largely royalist assembly, which hoped that the monarchy would eventually be restored. Both Flaubert and Turgenev found this regime antipathetic in the extreme, the latter frequently referring to it as a military dictatorship and virtual police state.

That winter, during the Parisian winter season, the two met often to discuss together Flaubert's satirical and political play *The Candidate*, which unfortunately turned out to be a notable theatrical flop in the spring of 1874.

For his own part, Turgenev was working on what was to be his last full-length novel, the writing of which turned out to be slower and more problematic than any of his previous works. Flaubert's *Temptation of Saint Anthony* was published in May 1874. Turgenev spared no effort in trying to ensure favourable reviews of his friend's work. He even supplied a list of addresses for review copies for Charpentier, Flaubert's publisher.

In the summer of 1875 came the terrible shock to Flaubert of the bankruptcy of his nephew Ernest Commanville, a timber merchant. He was devastated by this news, not only on his niece Caroline's account, for whom he had always had virtually paternal feelings, but also on his own. By the terms of Mme Flaubert's will, Croisset now belonged to her grand-daughter, Mme Commanville, her son's interest in the property being for his lifetime only. There was now a very real prospect of having to sell up the family home. The letters that Turgenev wrote to his friend during these troubled months have not survived, but none the less his involvement in Flaubert's dilemma is clearly reflected in the letters he wrote to mutual acquaintances at this time. In August he wrote to George Sand:

> I realise that there is in what Flaubert says the unconscious exaggeration of an impressionable, nervous man, who has been spoilt by a free and easy life; none the less I sense that this has been a blow – an even harsher one than even he realises. He has tenacity, but no energy, in the same way that he has self-esteem without being vain. This misfortune has cut through his soul like a knife through butter. I asked twice if I could go and see him at Croisset and he refused me.[1]

And the following month he wrote to Zola in the hope of rallying support to help their friend through the difficult months ahead:

> Poor Flaubert's morale is in an absolutely pitiful state: as you say, all his friends must gather round him this winter. . . . Fate is so abominably brutal to strike at the one man in the world who is least capable of making a living from his work.[2]

Croisset
5 June 1872

My dear friend,
   Here are my plans for the summer.
   Next week, I am going to Paris. On the 23rd I shall be in Vendôme, for the inauguration of the statue of Ronsard.[3] The mayor has invited me and I shall go, in order to see a town where people still care about literature. I even thought of writing a *speech* for the occasion, that I would have delivered in the open air, before the masses!!! It would have been a fine opportunity to denounce modern *crassness* and to exalt the things we love. But I have neither the concentration nore the strength to write such a piece properly.

In July I shall probably take my niece to Luchon, as her husband is unable to accompany her – so we shall not be able to see each other before the middle of August. I shall be in Paris at that time, and I'm counting on bringing you back here, to show you the surrounding district, and to read you the end of *Saint Anthony*, which is starting to bore me, and in particular to worry me. I am afraid that it is all empty rhetoric.

My *business affairs* have caused me a lot of anxiety. Are you like me? I prefer to let myself be robbed, rather than act in self-defence, it's not that I'm not interested, but it all bores and wearies me. When it's a question of money, disgust and rage seize hold of me and I go almost out of my mind. I mean this very seriously.

I thought of you amid all this murky business, and here's why. It has been found, that in my father's estate, there was a sum of fourteen thousand francs to be held in trust for me, I was in total ignorance of its existence, and it's all been squandered by a dear cousin who was handling our affairs. I thought immediately of a trip to Russia, this little windfall would have allowed me to travel about there with you. But I don't think I shall ever see a halfpenny of it.

Ah! Dear friend, how I should love to stretch out alongside you on your great haystacks! That would refresh my sad and singularly weary being. I am re-reading Plutarch, and . . . what else? That's all.

Nothing new 'on the horizon'. A very fine speech by Dupanloup[4] in praise of the arts. It's worth seeing.

Farewell, dear Turgenev. Look after your health and happiness, think of me and come back to us.

Your

G. Flaubert, who embraces you.

Moscow
26 June 1872

My dear friend,

You sent me your plans for the summer – here are mine.

N.B.   For the moment I am in Moscow, pinned down by a nasty attack of gout, which keeps me confined to my sofa. I wasn't really expecting it, after last October's violent attack – it's becoming too frequent and I'm getting too many congratulations along the lines of 'it's a guarantee of long life etc., etc.' Fortunately the attack isn't too bad, and I hope to be able to leave the capital of all the Russias on Sunday or Monday. Today is Wednesday.

I shall head straight for Paris, and from there to Touraine, to my daughter, who is about to make me a grandfather; and from there to

Valéry-sur-Somme, where I shall rejoin my old friends the Viardots. I shall see what's new, I shall work if I can, and then I shall go to Paris to look up a certain Flaubert, whom I love dearly, and with him, I shall go either to his place at Croisset, or to Mme Sand's at Nohant, where we are invited it seems. And then from October onwards – Paris. There you are!

Old age, my dear friend, is a great dull cloud that envelops the future, the present and even the past, which it makes more melancholy, covering our memories with fine cracks, like old porcelain. (I'm afraid I'm expressing myself badly, but never mind.) We must defend ourselves against this cloud! I think you don't do so enough. In fact I think a journey to Russia, the two of us together, would do you good. I've just spent four whole days, not on the top of a haystack, but wandering along the paths of an old country garden, full of rustic perfumes, strawberries, birds, sunshine and sleepy shadows, with two hundred acres of gently waving rye all around! It was superb! One becomes transfixed in a kind of feeling of gravity and immensity – and stupefaction – which has to do both with physical animal existence and with God. One comes out of it as if having been immersed in some sort of restorative bath. And then one gets on with everyday living again.

Don't let St Anthony lose heart. Let him carry on courageously to the end.

I know that you were present at a fine musical evening at Mme Viardot's. It seems that people liked it.

You didn't say anything about my picture.[5] Do you not like it – or haven't you seen it?

Farewell and goodbye my dear friend . . . Let us keep our chins up before the waves submerge us.

I give you a cordial embrace.

Your
I. Turgenev

Maison Ruhaut Saint-Valéry-sur-Somme
Tuesday, 30 July 1872

Where are you at the moment, my dear friend, and what are you doing between now and the winter? Send me a note, I beg you. As for me, I have been in this little hole, where I'm writing from, for two weeks, and I should find it perfectly agreeable, were it not for the damned gout that has got me by the leg again – and more obstinately than ever.

It seized hold of me six weeks ago in Moscow – and will not let go. I've had three or four relapses, I walked on crutches, then with two sticks – with one – and here I am, pretty well immobilised again. Old age is a dreadful thing – begging Cicero's pardon.

I am here with the Viardot family – I have a very nice room, where there is nothing to prevent me from working . . . but there you are! I doesn't come. There's rust on the springs.

And Anthony – what is he up to? Give me news of him.

This loan of 9, 12, 15 billions seems to me like a great burst of artillery fire.[6] You damned French never cease to amaze us in one way or another.

I have been a grandfather since the 18th; my daughter is delivered of a girl, whom they've called Jeanne – and to whose baptism I shall go towards the end of August. I shall have to go through Paris twice. If you were at Croisset then, I could carry on as far as your place.

So – keep well and goodbye! I give you a hearty shake of the hand.

Your

I. Turgenev

Bagnères-de-Luchon
Monday, 5 August [1872]

My dear Turgenev,

I shall be back in Paris next Friday; and three or four days later, I shall be back at Croisset *where I expect you*. I have to be away during the first few days of September. So don't come after the 25th at the latest.

I have the end of *Saint Anthony* to read to you. I'm afraid of having skimped on it, and there are so many things to talk to you about. I don't feel in very good form either. I am in a 'state of dryness' as the mystics say. I am without 'grace'.

It's hard to talk in Paris. The noise from the street and the nearness of Other People deprive one of any peace. Come to my old homestead then. We shall be completely alone, and we'll have a good chat.

Will you please give my respects to Mme Viardot? As for you, I embrace you.

Your

G. Flaubert

Don't think of treating your gout, poor dear friend. All remedies are dangerous. There's only one that I trust, and it's atrocious. I'll tell you about it. My blessings on the head of mademoiselle Jeanne.

Croisset
Thursday [29 August 1872]

I have been waiting for you here for two weeks, my dear friend. No Turgenev and no letters! Have you had another attack of gout? You were supposed to come here on the way to or back from your grandson's [*sic*] baptism.

I have to travel around *on business* until about 20 September. I shall pass through Paris. So write to me at 4 rue Murillo, in order that I might have your letter without delay. The one I sent you at Saint-Valéry was perhaps lost.

What an enormous quantity of things I have to tell you, and how I long to embrace you!

Your
G. Flaubert

I'm *counting* on seeing you here in October. Arrange things in advance so that you can stay a long time. I have some amusing things to show you.

Paris
13 September [1872]

I should have liked to have gone with you, my dear friend, and made the journey together to Nohant, but I must return to Croisset.

I expect you there towards 10 or 12 October, as you say. Organise yourself so as to be able to stay for a long time. *I need* to explain to you in great detail a plan for a book, and to see you and to talk about a host of things.

I shall be back at Croisset towards the 20th and shan't shift from there.

I embrace you.

Your
G. Flaubert

My most humble respects to Mme Viardot.

How I pity you in your ceaseless sufferings, poor dear friend! Let me have your news from time to time.

What fine literature the *Female Man* is.[7] Oh!

48 rue de Douai Paris
Monday, 7 October 1872

My dear friend,
    Let him who would congratulate me on having gout, adding that it is a guarantee of longevity, beware – he would surely risk hearing curses. Imagine, I have been in Paris for more than two weeks, and on the very day of my arrival I had a relapse (the eighth or ninth, I've lost count!) – and I have to stay in bed for a week without being able to move! Last Thursday, I make a superhuman effort – I go to Nohant – the whole Viardot family was there – I stay for a day, I come back, and here I am, confined to my bedroom again, limping wretchedly, and with no idea how long it will go on for! Never mind; I'm glad to have been to Nohant and to have seen Mme Sand at home, she is quite the best and kindest woman one can imagine! And her surroundings are charming.
    Now I must go to Croisset. But when? That's what I can't say, for certain. I know that I shall go as soon as I've rested a bit, very probably at the beginning of next week. I'll let you know in advance. I have the greatest desire to see you, to talk to you and to hear the ending of Anthony – and then it seems you have other plans. . . . So we must chat and gossip, it's an absolute necessity.
    In the meantime I embrace you and say goodbye.
                                    Your
                                        I. Turgenev

                                            Croisset
                    Saturday evening 19 [October 1872]

Well? What about the gout? Is it that, poor dear friend that's preventing you from coming? I fear it may have got worse.
    Should I still count on your visit? And when shall I see you? I have been expecting you every day since the beginning of the week.
    You will come, won't you?
                            All the best
                                G. Flaubert

                                48 rue de Douai Paris
                                    21 October 1872

My dear friend,
    I didn't reply straightaway to your first letter, because I wanted to be able to say when I should come and see you. Today I think I can at

last hope that the gout is leaving me, and that I shall be able to go to Croisset on Monday or Tuesday of next week. Before coming your way, I must go to a place near Châteaudun, to my daughter, who has blessed me with a granddaughter, whom I have not yet seen. In any case I'll send you a note the day before I set off for your place.

I don't need to tell you how much I'm longing to see you.

In the meantime I give you a friendly embrace.

Your

I. Turgenev

Croisset

Wednesday [23 October 1872]

Poor dear friend,

How I pity you in your incessant suffering! Physical pain 'whatever they say' is the worst thing in the world, since it interferes with our liberty. Those who bear it without complaint either don't feel it, or are liars.

As soon as it's left you and you can get on a train, come here, and arrange things so as to spend several days with me. If it's fine, I'll show you some amusing things in the surrounding district, and then we'll chat, that especially.

I advise you to take the afternoon express that leaves Paris at 12.55 p.m. Write to me and I'll come and meet you. I expect you towards the beginning of next week, as you said.

Your old man who loves you

G. Flaubert

48 rue de Douai Paris

Sunday, 27 October 1872

Dear friend,

On *Thursday* I went to see my daughter; I came back with great difficulty on *Friday* – I yelled with pain the whole of Friday night – today I am no longer in pain – but my knee is bigger than my head – and here I am in bed for two weeks at least. It's my *eleventh* attack of gout! You'll have to admit that I'm remarkably lucky.

So I have sworn not to move again before spring – when I shall go to take the waters at Carlsbad. For shame! Life is becoming too ugly – and it makes me really sick.

If you want to see me, you'll have to come to Paris. Come on 9 November – it's my birthday – and I promised Mme Viardot's daughters ages ago to give a little party on that day – although the way things are going, there is really no reason for me to rejoice in having been born that day. In any case there will be dancing downstairs, and we will chat upstairs, and I'll listen to a bit of Anthony (if you bring it, because I'm interested in it, in spite of all my sufferings and disgust).

Write me a note; I'm very depressed – but I embrace you affectionately.

> Your
> I. Turgenev

Croisset
Wednesday evening [30 October 1872]

How I pity you, poor dear friend. I didn't need to know that you are very ill in order to be sad. The death of dear old Theo[8] has shattered me. For the last three years, all my friends have been dying one after the other, without a break! There's only one man left in the world now with whom I can talk, and that's you. So you must look after yourself, so that I shan't miss you, along with the others.

Theo died poisoned by the filth of modern life. People who are exclusively artists, as he was, have no place in a society dominated by the rabble. That's what I said yesterday in a letter to Mme Sand, who is very good, but too good, too full of vain talk, too democratic and she evangelises too much.

I am feeling the same as you, Although I haven't got the gout; life is starting to get me down terribly. Voltaire said life is a sick joke. I'm finding it too sick and not at all funny; I try to keep the upper hand as much as possible: I read for about nine or ten hours a day; all the same, a bit of enjoyment from time to time wouldn't come amiss. But what kind of amusement should I try?

Your visit, on which I was counting, should have been an exquisite one, even more, a form of happiness, and certainly the only happy event in my year. And here you are, condemned to suffering in your bed!

You'll see me in Paris early in December. Let me have news of you between now and then, and if you are well enough to come, come. You will always be welcome at the house of your

> G. Flaubert who embraces you.

48 rue de Douai Paris
Friday, 8 November 1872

My dear friend,

We have been writing very sad letters to each other for some time now – there is illness and death in the air – it's not our fault – but we must try and shake ourselves a bit. I hardly knew Gautier at all – do you remember our dinner at your place? – but I was greatly upset to learn of his death; I thought of you at once, knowing how close you were to him. Mme Sand talks of you in a note I've just got from here; she's worried at seeing you in such a black state or mind, and tells me to try and cheer you up a bit. I don't know what I could say – but I know that a good long conversation would do us both good. Ah well! How are we going to manage this conversation? My damned gout seems to be loosening its grip on me, but I mustn't even think of travelling: I can walk, with a limp, without a stick, but I have not yet been out of my two rooms. So we must wait for your arrival here.

Why should you bother yourself so much about the *rabble*, as you call them? They only hold sway over those who accept their yoke. It really is a case of '*etiam si omnes, ego non*'. And then is M. Alexandre Dumas the younger – the embodiment of 'filth' to use your expression – one of the rabble? And M. Sardou, M. Offenbach, M. Vacquerie[9] and all the rest, are they part of the rabble? They stink none the less. So do the rabble – but they stink of Cambronne's word;[10] the others stink of putrefaction. And after all, as long as there is someone in the world who loves you and has a fellow feeling for you . . .

No my friend; it's not that that's difficult to bear at our age; it's the general '*taedium vitae*', the boredom and disgust with all human activity; it's nothing to do with politics, which after all is no more than a game; it's the sadness of one's fiftieth year. And that's why I admire Mme Sand: such serenity, such simplicity, such an interest in everything, such goodness! If for that one has to be a bit over idealistic, democratic or even evangelising – by God! – let's put up with such excesses.

You must come to Paris and bring Anthony – and then make plans, conquer the world! It's all very well out being sceptical, critical, worn out and tired, but poetry has got its bodkin in our backs, goading us on, and we must carry on the forward march, especially if one can be encouraged by the sight of one's comrade advancing at one's side.

'I'm not going to read over this allegorico-metaphorical letter; I don't really know what I've written – I know that I embrace you and that I'll see you soon.

Your
I. Turgenev

Croisset
Wednesday 13 [November 1872]

I found your last letter touching, my good Turgenev. Thank you for your encouragement! But alas, I fear that my sickness is incurable. Apart from personal sources of grief (the deaths, within the space of three years, of almost all those I loved), the *state of society is crushing me*. Yet, that's the way it is. It may be stupid. But there you are. I am overwhelmed by public Stupidity. Since 1870, I've been a patriot. Seeing my country die has made me realise that I loved it. Prussia may dismantle her guns. We don't need her to bring about our demise.

The bourgeoisie is so stunned that it no longer even has the instinct of self-preservation; and what will follow will be worse! I feel the same sadness experienced by Roman patricians in the fourth century. I feel a wave of relentless Barbarism, rising up from below the ground. I hope to be dead before all is swept away. But in the meantime, it is no joke. Never have affairs of the mind counted for less. Never have hatred of everything that is great, contempt for all that is beautiful, abhorrence for literature been so manifest.

I have always tried to live in an ivory tower; but a sea of shit is beating up against its walls, it's enough to bring it down. It's not a question of politics, but of the *mentality* prevalent in France. Have you seen Simon's[11] circular on the question of educational reform? The paragraph dealing with physical exercise is longer than the one devoted to French literature. This is a small symptomatic sign.

In fact, my dear friend, if you didn't live in Paris, I would immediately give up the lodgings I rent there. The hope of seeing you there sometimes is the only thing that makes me keep them on.

I can no longer talk with anyone without getting angry; and all the contemporary writing I read makes me wild. A fine state of affairs! – all of which doesn't stop me planning a book in which I shall try to spit out my rancour. I would really like to talk to you about it. So I am not admitting defeat as you see. If I didn't work there would be nothing for it but to throw myself into the river with a stone round my neck. 1870 drove many people into madness, imbecility or rage. I am in the last category. That's the truth.

The excellent Mme Sand is probably fed up with my ill humour. I hear nothing of her these days. When is her play being performed?[12] Isn't it at the beginning of December? It's about then that I hope to pay you a visit.

In the meantime, try to bear your gout, poor dear friend; and believe that I love you.

Your
G. Flaubert

48 rue de Douai Paris
11 December 1872

Well then! Here we are in the middle of December – and no Flaubert?
Unfortunately I am not like Muhammad – I cannot go to the mountain. I cannot go at all – for I have not been out of my bedroom these
last two weeks – and God knows how long this state of affairs will
continue! My gout is at least as obstinate as the Versailles assembly[13]
and I think it will persist even when the latter has dissolved itself, or
rather, has been dissolved. Come on now, make an effort and come to
Paris. Be sure to write to me if you're coming – and *when* is it to be? No
one has come – it's depressing, Mme Sand is staying at Nohant as well.
But I haven't given you up – I shall only say 'until we see each other'.
    In the meantime I embrace you.

Your
I. Turgenev

[Croisset]
12 December [1872]

My dear friend,
    I had at first planned to spend a fortnight in Paris at the beginning of
this month, then to come back here until the end of January. But at the
moment I can't bear the thought of being shunted around in railway
carriages; and in order to avoid all the coming and going, I decided to
sort out my *business matters* first!! And bring forward the date of my
winter season.
    So you won't see me before 15 January. When I've embraced you, I
shall go and see Mme Sand, who seems not to want to come to Paris
this winter, because her play isn't going to be produced. The censor
has banned it. I think that's monstrous! Oh what a fine state we're in!
Where will this excess of public stupidity end? . . .
    Poor dear friend, how upset I am to hear that you are still suffering!
You seem to be pretty fed up. A quarter of an hour of my company
wouldn't be likely to cheer you up. I'm in a Funereal frame of mind.
    I really feel like a good long talk with you, especially about the book
I'm pondering on. It's going to involve me in a lot of reading. But
when I've vomited my gall, perhaps I shall feel more settled.
    The *Nouvelliste de Rouen* printed your 'King Lear of the Steppe' at
the beginning of November. It was a tribute to you on the part of the
editor who knew you were supposed to be visiting me then.
    In about six weeks then, we shall see each other at last.

Tibissimi
G. Flaubert

12 December, my birthday. Your friend is now 51 years old, and has no wish to see this figure doubled, contrary to the sentiments always expressed in drunken wedding songs:

In a hundred years' time
May we gaily rhyme
  Love your love
  Love your love   repeat

The 'love' is the young woman with whom it is considered by the assembled company that the singer has 'had his way'. Charming! Charming!

[Paris]
Wednesday evening [January 1873]

My dear friend,
    You haven't heard from me, because I have a dreadful attack of the 'flu. I am at the *coughing* stage, which is the worst for other people. How much longer will it go on for? There's the problem! As soon as I'm better, I'll come and see you.
    How wonderful 'King Lear of the Steppe' is. I can't wait to talk to you about it.

Your old
G. Flaubert

who is not weeping for Badinguet[14] although it is the thing to do.

Paris
Thursday evening 10 o'clock [13 March 1873]

My dear friend,
    Mme Commanville, my niece, lives at 77 rue de Clichy.
    It's still not possible to say when I shall be able to read *Saint Anthony* to you, and it's not that I don't want to, since at present you are the *only human being* I esteem, the only real writer in existence, the only friend I have left. But my larynx is far too damaged to be able to yell out appropriately for several hours at a stretch.
    Another idea. If you are coming with me to Nohant, wouldn't it be better to wait until we're at Nohant, since I've got to read *Saint Anthony* to Mme Sand? Otherwise, you'd hear the thing three times, which I think would be a bit much.

As soon as I can go out, I'll come and see you. In any case, try to come and see me next Sunday afternoon.

All the best.

> *Ex imo*
> G. Flaubert

> Paris
> Tuesday [Spring 1873]

My dear friend,

Do you know Mme Ernesta Grisi, Théo's[15] former mistress and the mother of his children? Probably not. Never mind, here is the favour I'm going to ask you on her behalf. She came to see me on Sunday to tell me she's going to hold a concert on the 19th of this month, in order to raise a little money; because she's dying of poverty; and she begged me to ask Mme Viardot to sing at it. I told her that I don't know Mme Viardot sufficiently well to ask her such a thing. I don't like making myself disagreeable to no purpose.

However, if I were sure that Mme Viardot would not refuse my request, I would ask her. Could you try and find out tactfully if she would agree to do such a charitable deed, and let me know what she wants to do about it.

I thought I should see you last Sunday, either at my place or at the 'unmentionable' house.[16] Shall I see you there tomorrow night? In any case, I hope to see you soon.

> Your old
> G. Flaubert

> 48 rue de Douai Paris
> Wednesday morning [Spring 1873]

My dear friend,

I have spoken to Mme V. on the subject of Mme E. Grisi's request. Unfortunately it's impossible. Mme V. has had to make a rule about not singing for private individuals: she gets so many requests, that if she once says yes, she won't ever be able to say no. She is particularly sorry not to be able to help in this case. When she was younger, it was all right, but now of course she has to be more careful. This is, my good friend, the exact truth.

I shall certainly come on Sunday, perhaps before. I shall probably go to Princess Mathilde's this evening.

A thousand friendly greetings from your

> I. Turgenev

[Nohant]
Monday evening, 4 o'clock [14 April 1873]

My dear friend,
We await you. They despair of seeing you. I maintain that you will come. There's the problem!
At Châteauroux station, as you get off the train, you'll find carriages for hire. Take one. There is of course the stage coach, but your size does not permit you to travel in that packing case.
I still intend to leave here on Saturday.
Do come, otherwise you are a man whose word is not his bond.
Your old
Gustave Flaubert who embraces you

Croisset
Thursday [29 May 1873]

I received your new book the day before yesterday, my dear friend.[17] I'm not saying anything about it, because I haven't read it yet. I shall tackle it when I have sorted out my first act a bit more. Give me your address in Carlsbad, so that I can write to you. I'm working like a mad thing on *The Weaker Sex*,[18] a wretched task on the whole. Nevertheless, I think I'll be able to make something of it.
It's filthy weather here, I haven't even been as far as the bottom of my garden yet. I'm having my poor old house done up, so as to be worthy to receive you, when you come here on your return, (i) to here me read *The Weaker Sex* and my fairy piece[19] and (ii) to visit the surrounding district.
I embrace you.
Your old
G. Flaubert

Present my humble respects to Mme Viardot.

Croisset near Rouen
Saturday [31 May 1873]

I couldn't hold out, my dear friend! I opened your book, in spite of my solemn oaths to be good. And I devoured its contents.
What a fantastic fellow you are! I'm not talking about 'Lear of the Steppe' which I knew already, but about 'Knock . . . Knock . . . Knock. . .' and especially about 'The Unfortunate Girl'. I don't know

if you've ever shown greater skill as a poet and psychologist. It's marvellous, a masterpiece. Such artistry! What cunning devices in the writing of it, underneath the simple straightforward appearance!

These are the thoughts that come to mind.

In 'Knock . . . Knock . . . Knock . . .', the creation of Teglev, the instrument of fate, who is a poseur and yet at the same time naïve! (His letter! His sacred album!) And the fog when they are searching for him! You can feel the cold in your bones. You can see it all! Or rather you can feel it! The suspense is sustained throughout the mystery, so as to make one almost afraid. Then the explanation comes along quite naturally and relieves the tension.

The first of your stories is the one I liked least. The second scene, the landscape in the rain has strength, none the less; but I think you could have filled the whole thing out rather more. Isn't it a bit short? Perhaps I'm being stupid.

But I'm sure I'm not being in stating that 'The Unfortunate Girl' is a work of first-class quality. The clinging young man who is afraid of compromising himself, the Jew and his family, young Victor, and especially her, your unfortunate girl I found enchanting. I let out cries of delight in my armchair. It does one good to have something to admire!

The description of the way Susanna plays the piano, the portrayal of her father, the old gentleman etc., etc. What can I say? You simply amaze me! Such things defy analysis.

There is a sentence (just a minute while I look for the book) it's page 269: 'and like those pinpoints of light moving in the darkness, I felt my own inner shadows pierced by a sudden and unfamiliar brightness' that I find of a rare precision and beauty. And how clever, from the point of view of keeping the interest going, to have given no details about her relationship with her second lover, who was of course her only lover. Thanks to the removal of the last pages of the manuscript, she remains pure in the reader's memory.

But what beats all is the burial, the children lifted up over the corpse, the final drunkenness. Great, my dear friend, great!

As for me, I'm not involved in such high literature at the moment. I'm working on *The Weaker Sex*. I've still got about a month or three weeks to go on it, not more. It's true that I work long days, and that I stick at it frenetically without a break.

Where are you now? Give me news of Mme Viardot.

I embrace you heartily.

Your
Gve Flaubert who loves you

48 rue de Douai Paris
Wednesday, 4 June 1873

My dear friend,

Can you imagine me not being as proud as a peacock after all you say to me in your letter!! I shall guard that one preciously. Truly, you have given me great pleasure, and I'm happy to see that I gave you pleasure also. I shake your hand heartily.

You are right to find the first piece ('A Strange Story') rather abridged. It needed much greater development – those are psychological states that can't just be sketched in. But I was lazy!

I am still here – but I leave tomorrow. I shall write to you from Vienna and certainly from Carlsbad.

Work hard – no, there is no need to say that to you – you labour like an ant, but keep well and expect me at Croisset in early August.

All the family are well and they send you their best wishes.

I embrace you heartily and am for every your old.

Iv. Turgenev

P.S.   You will receive my other book as soon as it comes out. I am rather anxious about this one.[20]

Croisset near Rouen
Thursday [19 June 1873]

It is agreed and *sworn on*, is it not, my dear friend? If I am not in Paris at the end of July, you will take devotion so far as to come to my old homestead for a while.

You are right to love me, for I love you dearly. *I'm dying* to have boundless conversations with you, and I embrace you.

G. Flaubert

Croisset
Thursday, 10 July [1873]

My dear friend,

Where are you, and how are you? Mme Sand wrote to me that you had had a fall and hurt your leg. That's all I know. Put my mind at rest and let me have news of you.

You know I'm counting on your promise, that is, I expect you here at the beginning of August. I say at the very beginning because from about the 8th or 10th I have to be away until the end of the month.

I embrace you.

Your old

G. Flaubert

Croisset
31 July [1873]

Ah! At last! I have news of my good old Turgenev, and he sends me a book by him, thus promising me a day of rare pleasure.

But this is what has happened, my dear friend: I have to leave here next Tuesday or Wednesday at the latest. Now as I mean to keep you here *for a long time*, because i) I have loads of things to read to you, and ii) I want to show you the surrounding district, I'd rather you come at the beginning of September. At the moment you wouldn't be able to stay long enough to satisfy my thirst for your company.

Mme Sand had made me anxious about your fall, but I see that all is well. So much the better. Keep in good health for those who love you and don't want to see you suffering.

I'm expecting Carvalho esquire next Saturday, and on Sunday I shall have Raoul-Duval[21] here. We should have no peace. However, if you can't come in September, come straightaway, because a little is better than none at all. But I would prefer September.

I am in a dramatic vein, for I have finished *The Weaker Sex*, and planned a great political comedy called *The Candidate*, which hasn't stopped me getting on with the reading for my two old fellows.[22]

I am going off to Dieppe, Trouville and then to Paris and district.

Drop me a line to let me know your plans.

Say nice things to the Viardots on my behalf. As for you, my dear old man, I embrace you as strongly as is possible.

Gve Flaubert

who is going to bed down on his divan and get stuck in to *Spring Torrents*.

[Croisset]
Saturday 2 [August 1873]

It's me again, dear fellow!

I want to tell you that I've read *Spring Torrents* and re-read *Lear of the Steppe* of which I didn't know the second part.

Spring Torrents didn't bowl me over like *The Unfortunate Girl*; but I was moved by it, tears came to my eyes, and I felt a certain pressure from within. It's the story of us all, alas! It makes one blush on one's own account. What a man my friend Turgenev is! What a man!

The interior of the sweet shop, adorable! adorable! And the morning walk the two of them have, when they chat on a bench. Pantaleone, the poodle; Aeneas! And the ending, the gentle, sad ending!

Ah! that's a love story if ever there was one. You know a lot about life, my dear friend, and you know how to express what you know, which is rarer.

I'd like to be a teacher in a grammar school, in order to give lessons on your books. But note that I wouldn't explain them at all. Never mind, I think I could make even an idiot understand certain devices that take my breath away. For example: the contrast between your two women in *Spring Torrents* and that between their surroundings.

To describe your latest work, I can find no other word than this, which is a silly one: *charming*. But take it in its true sense, which is profound. It puts love into your heart: you smile and feel like crying.

The beginning of *Lear* is quite amusing. That stupid rage fixes the character very well. This story, like all good books, gains from a second reading.

So, I expect you about 10 September. We shall not be bored when we are together.

Greetings to your friends. And to you, my dear old fellow, all my deepest tenderness.

G. Flaubert

Maison Halgan Bougival (Seine-et-Oise)
Wednesday, 6 August 1873

You say too many kind things, my dear friend; they make me blush with pleasure – and embarrassment. But it's all the same, it's very pleasant, and the old Romans were right when they spoke of '*laudari a laudato viro*'.[23]

I am so pleased and so proud to have given pleasure to my old Flaubert – and to the author of *Anthony*. And it is very kind of him to have said all that.

My letter will perhaps find you not at Croisset – but never mind. It must go. On 10 September I shall come and we won't be bored – oh no!

Did you know that the whole band of us (I'm talking about my friends here, who want to be remembered to you) is going to Nohant at the end of September, for a week at least! Why don't you come too – that would be marvellous!

It is abominably hot – and in spite of having the shutters closed, I'm more or less soaking wet. Writing is a heroic act in such conditions – so you will permit me to kiss you on both cheeks and to say goodbye and once again thank you.

Your old faithful
Iv. Turgenev

[Paris]
Monday 25 [August 1873]

My good old Turgenev,

I've been in Paris for a few days already, but I'm so busy that it won't be possible to come and see you at Bougival, as I intended.

It's you who will come and see me at Croisset, as we agreed. My niece wrote to me this morning that she's counting on seeing you at Dieppe. So, dear friend, make your arrangements beforehand.

I have several things to read to you and I want to take you out a bit. All this will need several days. Arrange things so that you can stay with me a long time. It is 10 September that you're coming, isn't it?

I embrace you.

Your

G. Flaubert

You can answer me this week in Paris. Then I shall be at Saint-Gratien, then near Rambouillet for *B. and P.*, finally back at Croisset on the 7th or 8th, where I shall await you impatiently.

Maison Halgan Bougival (Seine-et-Oise)
Thursday 28 August 1873

My dear friend,

Dead or alive, I shall come to Croisset – but here is what has happened.

Two years ago, in England, I met a very pleasant young man called Bullock[24] who had an extremely rich uncle, an old retired general, called Hall. This General Hall owned the finest partridge shoot in the whole of England!!! – no less. But he was an eccentric who hunted alone and only ever invited his nephew – from time to time. And now he had died and left his fortune, his name and his *shoot* to his nephew; and so the nephew has remembered me and has invited me to go and kill *mountains* of partridges between the 9th and 14th September! Despite my unbridled passion for hunting, the only passion left to me, I remembered my promise – and I replied . . . evasively; the more so as I don't know if my gout will allow me to get up to such pranks – and if it is not shameful for an old fogey like me to cross the seas twice over to go and shoot lead at partridges? The thing is, I can't make up my mind – and that's why, wanting to feel at ease about it, I'm asking you to put back my arrival at Croisset 5 days. That is, to come on the 15th instead of the 10th. It's more than likely that I shan't go to England – but like that, there's no problem. It's agreed then?

I have to go to Paris on Saturday on business. At midday exactly, I shall be in the Café Riche having lunch. If you could come – wonderful! If not, I know you will agree to this little delay without offence.

In the meantime I wish you good health and good humour – and I embrace you.

Your

I. Turgenev

[Croisset]

Thursday [25 September 1873]

Ah! At last!!!

So, *I expect you next week,* on condition though that you don't leave too soon. Make arrangements beforehand. I also have lots to tell you.

We shall see if 'Gaultier d'Aulnay is a man of no faith nor honour' (*Tour de Nesle*).[25]

I embrace you, *burning* with impatience.

Your

G. Flaubert

48 rue de Douai Paris

Wednesday 19 November 1873

Well, dear friend, since yesterday evening you have a military dictatorship. You are, as they say, Macmahonites.[26] It had always seemed to me that it was better simply to be French; but perhaps I'm wrong.

The only good thing about all this, is that nothing should now stand in the way of your publishing 'Anthony', since we've been promised peace, an upturn in business and for seven whole years. I went to Versailles the day before yesterday and came back quite disgusted and saddened.

The devil take politics! I'm very pleased to see that you're working hard and that your comedy is making great strides forward. Sardou's (that I haven't seen by the way) is creating more noise than anything else. I don't think it will make the two hundred performances of *Rabagas*.[27] Yours might be on before then.

My health is better, I'm a bit troubled by a nervous cough, but I suppose we've got to have something.

I'm not leaving Paris before the end of January. I hope to see you soon. Everyone is well.

I embrace you.

Your old

Iv. Turgenev

[Croisset]
Wednesday evening 3 December [1873]

I've finished *The Candidate*! Carvalho came to hear me read it on Sunday, and I go into rehearsal on the 20th of this month.

But . . . but . . . After all, my dear old fellow, I'm a bit worried and apprehensive about all that I shall have to go through. Never have anything to do with the theatre! A day such as I spent on Sunday is like nothing on earth. My nerves aren't strong enough for me to survive in those circles.

In short, you'll see me in less than two weeks. So don't leave so soon. Are you seriously going to set off for Russia right in the middle of such a cold spell? (If cold can have a middle.)

Re-reading your letter of 19 November, I see that you aren't to leave 'our shores' before the end of January. So much the better. We shall have time to see each other a bit. I'm quite impatient to read my play to you.

Carvalho wants me to include violence in it, tirades against . . . goodness knows what – the popular press for example – which I have refused categorically, because I think all that is facile, cheap and it offends my aesthetic sense, to be frank, it's unworthy of me.

Good old Carvalho, who is used to people who take no more trouble over their work than a bootmaker, cannot understand my finer feelings. I'm sure he left here thinking me three parts mad. Indeed, I am not 'reasonable'; I don't do things 'like everybody else'. Hence the shock and the scandal.

Oh! Action! As soon as I have anything to do with it, I'm in trouble. And then there is a maxim of Epictetus that one shouldn't forget: 'If you seek to please, you will be undone.'

If you have nothing better to do, send me a sample of your handwriting. That would be kind.

I embrace you as I love you, very vigorously.

Your
G. Flaubert

My niece is in Sweden with her husband. She'll be in Paris towards the New Year.

Respects and greetings to all at your place.

48 rue de Douai Paris
Saturday 6 December '73

My dear friend, if I didn't reply to you sooner, it was because I've been away for three days at my daughter's. I'm very pleased to hear that you've finished your play – and not at all surprised that Carvalho wants to chop and change things. There will be more of the same – you should '*steel' your nerves* for it now – as the Germans say – simply because your play isn't like the run of the mill. The essential thing is to come through all these birth pangs as calmly as possible.

I look forward to seeing you soon – I'm not leaving Paris for at least two months – or even longer.

I haven't seen *Uncle Sam*[28] yet, but I've seen Dumas's *M. Alphonse*. It's *very well constructed* – and all in all quite remarkable and gripping, although there is a part for an eleven-year-old girl that makes one sick and one finds sentences such as:

'Oh human heart, deep as the sky, as mysterious as the sea (or death!)' – or
'God's creature, vibrant being, where can I find the strength to punish you?' – or
'What was God's benevolence doing when he created this man?'

Can you imagine anything sillier?

All are well here; I went and knocked on Mme Commanville's door, only to find that she was in Stockholm. Paris is the place to be!

I shall see you soon, shan't I? I embrace you.

Your

Iv. Turgenev

[Paris]
[8 March 1874]

My good fellow,

The first night is on Wednesday, and the dress rehearsal on Tuesday at 12.30 p.m.

So far I haven't got a box for you. (Oh what trouble I've had over the seats!) But I have *three* seats in the stalls. My niece has only got a box in the upper circle.

I've had to put up 228 francs, and my friends can't get seats or only bad ones.

G. Flaubert

Hotel de St Petersburg Berlin
Sunday 17 May 1874

My dear friend,

I'm sending you an article on Anthony that has just appeared in the *Nationalzeitung*. It's by K. Frenzel – and on the whole it is quite favourable. But why haven't the copies I asked for been sent to Julian Schmidt who is the top literary critic in Germany, and to Louis Pietsch who is the top serialiser? I am *absolutely sure* that I included them on my list. Have this omission rectified as soon as possible. Here are the addresses again:

Dr Julian Schmidt, Kurfürstenstrasse no.70, Berlin

Mr Ludwig Pietsch, Landgrafenstrasse no.8, Berlin

I've seen both of them, and they both complained of having received nothing.

I'm sending this letter to Paris, because I suppose you are still there: but if you are not, it will be forwarded.

I'm leaving this evening for Petersburg. I dine there the day after tomorrow, all being well. My address at St Petersburg is Hotel Demouth.

I embrace you cordially.

Your old
I. Turgenev

Croisset
1 June [1874]

My dear old fellow,

I was stupid enough to lose your letter from Berlin, in which you gave me your address at Saint Petersburg, so that this will be forwarded on to you by Mme Viardot to whom I am sending it.

How many kilometres there are between us! But the proverb is true: 'Absence makes the heart grow fonder.' I had proof of it in your kindness in sending me a favourable review of *Saint Anthony*.

It seems ages since I had news from you. If you have time, write me a long letter.

As for me, dear friend, here is my programme: towards the end of the month, I'm going for a change of air to the Rigi for about three weeks. I shall spend a few days in Paris; then I shall come back here to settle down to my novel which makes me tremble more and more. The more I think about it, the more panic builds up.

As Perrin[29] didn't want *The Weaker Sex*, I've taken it to the Odeon, but I haven't heard from them yet. I'm not really very bothered about it now, having become completely philosophical as far as the theatre is concerned.

This very day, I've just read Zola's latest novel *La Conquête de Plassans* in one sitting, and I'm still completely dazed by it. It's strong stuff. It's better than *Le Ventre de Paris*. Towards the end there are one or two superb touches. Mme Sand has sent me *Sister Jeanne*, which I shall start tomorrow. But I have so much to read (for my book) that my poor eyes are starting to tire. I need to know just about everything for that devil of a book.

Have you found the information you needed for yours at Saint Petersburg? As for me, I've still had no luck in deciding where to set the house of my two old fellows. In two weeks' time, I shall go for a trip round Lower Normandy for this express purpose. Shall I be any happier? *Things aren't going well*. It seems to me at times that I'm empty. I'm experiencing what the mystics call a state of dryness. I have got no confidence. First sign of decrepitude. Oh! If only we could shake off our old skin like snakes do, renew our spirit, be rejuvenated!

What's the weather like over there? Here it's very hot, and the Parisians are panting. Summer is a season that brings out the ridiculous in people. Why? I've no idea. But there it is.

What about your gout? And your stomach? And the rest of you, what are you doing?

My niece, who is now at Croisset, asks me to send you her best wishes. She is leaving for Sweden in about ten days' time. The trip to Russia is still not settled.

Adieu, my dear and good old fellow. Keep your spirits up and look after your health. I embrace you tenderly.

Your

G. Flaubert

Send me your next letter at Croisset, up until about 20 June. And in your plans, don't forget that you've promised to come here and spend *at least* a fortnight in the autumn. Charpentier confirms that he had sent copies of *Saint Anthony* 'to all the addresses given by Mr Turgenev'.

Spasskoye Mtsensk Province of Oryol
Wednesday 17 June 1874

My dear friend,
I'm writing to you from my depths of the backwoods, where I arrived this morning, and where I found your letter of 1 June. It took

its time – as you see – but it's not its fault, nor Mme Viardot's. I didn't expect to stay so long in Petersburg and Moscow – I had given an itinerary – or rather a timetable that turned out to be inaccurate. What's annoying is that you'll no longer be at Croisset as from the 20th – that's the day after tomorrow – and that this letter will have to chase after you. It will catch up with you I'm sure, but nevertheless that thought inhibits my pen just a little.

It's not the first time I've written to you from here – and you know what it's like: it's green and gold, vast, monotonous, gentle, old fashioned and terribly static. A slow patriarchal boredom that's all enveloping. If I can manage to work, I shall stay here for a few weeks, otherwise I'll be off with all speed to Carlsbad – and from there to Paris. In any case, my stay in Russia has not been in vain, I found more or less what I was looking for; it's true that I am less – much less – demanding than you; you are too much that way. You are pleased with Zola's novel? I have written to him; I have arranged things for him for the future – it's not much, but it's better than nothing.[30] He continues to be widely read in Russia – and translated; his *Curée* has just come out.

'Anthony' is decidedly not something for a mass audience: ordinary readers shy away from it in horror – even in Russia. I didn't think that my compatriots were as finicky as that. It doesn't matter. For Anthony – in spite of everything – is a book that will survive.

I've got quite a few things to tell you that will make you laugh when I get back, and we're in your study at Croisset. There are some curious – and interesting – things in my *'cara patria'*. At the moment, a slight excess of dairy produce – which I thought it safe to indulge in, hoping that my native air would cure all – has left me with the most violent colic!! I think it must be possible to detect it in the very shape of the words and letters that I write . . . That is neither curious nor interesting – what a damned stomach!

And what damned politics these days!!? Eh? What do you say? Neither you nor I like talking about it – but how can one not at least say Oh! and Ah!

I think with pleasure of the days when we can start up again our pleasant little dinners for heckled playwrights. In the meantime, if this letter finds you perched on the top of some glacier in the Rigi, profit fully from the change of air!

When you write to your niece, who is most kind, send her my best regards. I see that I shan't be seeing her in Russia.

Study of a compatriot seen from behind (16 June in a temperature of 16 degrees [Réaumur]).

Thereupon (not on this backside) I embrace you and say goodbye.

Your old

Iv. Turgenev

Kaltbad Rigi Switzerland
Thursday 2 July 1874

I am also hot, and I have the advantage or disadvantage over you that I am bored to tears. I came here as an act of obedience, because everyone said that the pure mountain air would decongest me and calm my nerves. Amen to that. But so far, I only feel completely bored, owing to the solitude and idleness; and then I am not a *child of Nature*: 'her wonders' move me less than those of the Arts. She crushes me without inspiring any 'great thoughts' in me. I feel like saying to her inside myself: 'It's all very fine. I came from you just a while ago, in a few moments I shall return thence; leave me alone, I need other amusements.'

The Alps, moreover, are out of proportion to man's being. They're too big to be of any use. This is the third time that they have provoked an unpleasant reaction in me. I hope it's the last. And then my companions, my dear fellow, these foreigners in the hotel! All German or English, armed with walking-sticks and eye-glasses. Yesterday I very nearly embraced three calves I met in a meadow through fellow feeling and the need to let myself go.

My journey got off to a bad start, as I had a tooth extracted at Lucerne by a local practitioner of that art. A week before setting off for Switzerland I went for a trip round the Orne and the Calvados and I finally found the place where I shall set my two old fellows. I'm impatient to be getting on with that book, which makes me terribly afraid, in anticipation.

You talk of *Saint Anthony* and say that the general public is not on his side. I knew that in advance, but I did expect to be better understood by the educated public. Without Drumont and little

Pelletan, I wouldn't have had any favourable reviews. I don't see any coming from Germany. Never mind! May God's grace prevail; what is done is done, and then as long as you like the work, I am paid in full. I haven't had any big successes since *Salammbô*. The failure of *Sentimental Education* is what weighs on my heart; I am amazed that they didn't understand that book.

I saw good old Zola last Thursday and he gave me news of you (for your letter of the 27th [*sic*] caught up with me in Paris the following day). Except for you and me, no one had said anything to him about *La Conquête de P.*, and he hasn't had any reviews, either good or bad. Times are hard for the Muses. Paris moreover seemed flatter and more stupid than ever. However detached we both may be from politics, we cannot help groaning at it, if only through physical disgust.

Ah, my dear good old Turgenev, how I wish it were autumn, so as to have you at Croisset for a good two weeks! You'll bring your work, and I'll show you the first pages of *B. and P.* which, let us hope, will be written, and then I'll listen to you.

Where are you presently, in Russia or at Carlsbad? What would be sublime would be to return to France via the Rigi. But there are no more Deciuses in this world.[31] I'm resisting the temptation to take a boat back down the lake and cross the St Gothard to go and finish my month in Venice. I could enjoy myself there at least.

My niece must be beyond Stockholm at the moment; she counts on being back at Dieppe at the end of July.

In order to keep myself busy, I'm going to try and get into two very obscure subjects. But I know myself, and I shall do absolutely nothing here. One needs to be twenty here and walk out with one's sweet heart. The chalets that are reflected in the water are love-nests. How one could hold her in one's arms on the edge of the precipices! How one could let oneself go, lying in the grass to the sound of waterfalls, with blue in one's heart and above one's head. But all this is no longer for the likes of us, old fellow, and hardly ever was for me.

I repeat, it is atrociously hot, the mountains with their summits covered in snow are dazzling. Phoebe's arrows flash by. The travellers sweat and drink, cooped up in their rooms. The amount that is eaten and drunk in Helvetia is frightful. There are bars and eating places everywhere. The domestics in Kaltbad are dressed impeccably; black suits from 7 o'clock in the morning; and as there are a great many of them, one has the impression of being served by a body of lawyers or a crowd of mourners at a funeral; it makes one think of one's own, very gay.

Write to me often and at length; for me your letters will be 'a drop of water in the desert'.

I expect to leave Switzerland towards the 15th; I shall doubtless spend a few days in Paris.

Adieu, dear great friend, I embrace you with all my strength.

Your

G. Flaubert

Prechistensky Boulevard Moscow
Sunday 12 July 1874

My dear friend,

I received your letter from the Rigi just as, supported painfully on two crutches, I was heaving myself into a carriage to leave the country and come here. I have not broken any limbs, as you might imagine; but my *native air*, that does so much good to the inhabitants of Marseilles, has brought on another attack of gout – and this time in *both* feet; it kept me in bed for two weeks and has still not left me. To say that all this makes me look at life through rose-tinted spectacles – or under blue skies (I'm thinking of your dream under the Swiss sky) – would be to tell a great lie. Illnesses, a cold, slow disgust, painful stirrings of useless memories are, my dear fellow, all that await us once we're past the age of fifty. And beneath and beyond all that – resignation, HIDEOUS resignation, that prepares the way for death . . . Enough! I'm going to try and get off to Karlsbad as soon as I can – not the K. where you're bored to death – but Karlsbad in Bohemia, where I shall stay for five weeks. And in the autumn – we'll see later! I don't want to make any plans for the moment – especially not anything to look forward to – I would be afraid of putting a jinx on myself.

You don't sound as if you're enjoying yourself very much on those *sublime* peaks, celebrated by Haller and Rousseau! One must admit that those who live constantly in the sight of those sublimities – I mean the Swiss – are the most boring and least-gifted people I know. 'Where does this anomaly spring from?' a philosopher would ask. Or perhaps it isn't an anomaly at all? What would Bouvard and Pécuchet's opinion be?

I am delighted that you have at last found a *setting* – or rather – *the* setting. But the more I think about it – the more I see it as a subject to deal with *presto* in the manner of Swift or Voltaire. You know that has always been my opinion. The plan you told me about seemed charming and funny. If you make it heavy, if you are too learned . . .

Anyway, you've made a start, you're kneading the dough.

Zola's *Conquête de Plassans* has been translated and abridged in a Russian journal. Later it will be translated in full. He is liked in Russia.

What about taking advantage of your glacier in the Rigi to create something passionate, torrid, incandescent? Eh? That's an idea!

But profit especially from the change of air. Unfortunately, in some people, boredom whips up and agitates the blood. Come back to us pale and monochrome, like a line of Lamartine.

I have good news from my friends in Paris and Bougival. That makes my blood run warmer.

On the question of politics . . .

You will be governed by a fine inglorious sabre, a policeman's sabre for seven years. And you'll see that it will end up governing on its own, without the assemblies.

That reminds me, that in the country (where I have a very good library) I read in a collection called 'Selected Speeches Delivered in the French Parliament from 1789–1825' Robespierre's discourse on the subject 'Should Louis XVI be tried?' – it seemed to me very fine! Later on towards the end of his career Robespierre spoiled himself: he became sentimental and full of great emotive booming phrases. But there was some good in that lad!

Goodbye my friend – probably until Croisset in September, with the two of us in good health, let us hope!

I embrace you.

Your old

Iv. Turgenev

P.S.   Are you sure it's Karlsbad that you're at? You twice write Karltbad; but that's an impossible name. I'll make a note on the address.

Dieppe

Wednesday 25 July 1874

My good old Turgenev,

I shall be back at Croisset on Friday (the day after tomorrow) and on Saturday 1 August I at last start *Bouvard and Pécuchet*! I have taken a vow! There's no going back! But how scared I am! I'm on ten-terhooks! I feel as if I were setting off on a very long journey into unknown territory, and that I shan't come back.

In spite of the immense respect I have for your critical judgement (for in you the critic is on the same level as the Creator, which is saying a lot) I don't share your opinion as to how the subject should be dealt with. If it's done briefly, with a concise, light touch, it will be a more or less witty fantasy, but will lack impact and verisimilitude, whereas if it's detailed and developed, it will look as though I believe in my story, and it can become a serious and even a frightening thing. The great danger is monotony and boredom. That's what I'm afraid of, however . . . but then, I can always tighten it up or abridge it later. Moreover, it's impossible for me to produce anything short. I can't express an idea without going the whole way.

Something else. Do you remember a play by me and Bouilhet: *The Weaker Sex*? Well, after being accepted by the Vaudeville and reworked by me, the Vaudeville changed its mind, then Perrin turned it down on the grounds of indecency, Duquesnel said it would have to be 'completely rewritten', the Cluny Theatre finds it excellent and the manager of these inferior boards counts on making a lot of money with it. Admire the contradictions in all these judgements! What do you say to all these fools, these highly experienced cretins? And how to draw any practical conclusion from their opinions! And to think that Mme Sand believes these men and listens to their views! In any case, the play will go on after Zola's,[32] probably in November. So I shall be in rehearsal towards the middle of October. That'll make me lose two months and perhaps bring me more insults. But I don't care in the least. The shortest sentence of *B. and P.* worries me more than the whole of *The Weaker Sex* put together.

Your last letter seems tinged with melancholy? If I let myself go, I could reply in similar vein. Because I also feel terribly fed up with everything, and mainly with myself. At times I think I'm going mad, that I have no ideas left, and that my skull is like an empty beer jug. My stay (or rather my crass idleness) at the Rigi has stupefied me. One should never rest, for from the moment one stops doing things, one things about oneself and becomes ill, or one thinks one's ill, which is the same thing.

And you, my poor old fellow? How is the gout? Since Karlsbad did you a lot of good last year why shouldn't it be the same this year?

If you come back towards the beginning of September, it's possible I might see you in Paris, as I shall be there for two or three days then. Otherwise I'm counting on you this autumn at Croisset. My book will be started and we'll be able to talk about it until we've exhausted every possibility.

Politics are becoming incomprehensibly stupid. I don't believe that the Assembly will be dissolved. On the subject of politics I saw a curious thing in Geneva: old Gaillard's beer shop, he who was a bootmaker and former general of the Commune. I'll describe it to you. *It's another world*, the world dreamed of by democracy, and which I shall never see, thank God. What will dominate for the next two to three centuries is enough to make a man of taste vomit. It's time we went.

Adieu, my good dear old fellow. Send me your news and come back cured.

I embrace you vigorously.

> Your
>
> G. Flaubert

Croisset
Tuesday 22 [September 1874]

Do send me your news, my dear old fellow. It's a month now since I heard anything from you, and I am afraid you may be too ill to write. As for me, for several days I've had violent dysentery which I've managed to cure with bismuth and laudanum.

I feel more confident about *Bouvard and Pécuchet* now. It's going better. I think I'm getting it about right. I shall soon have finished the first chapter.

The rehearsals for *The Weaker Sex* will doubtless begin in a month's time. So I'll come to Paris about then for the whole winter; but between now and then I should like to have finished the introduction to my two old fellows.

As you are a reader of Buloz's rag, did you savour *The Story of a Diamond* by P. de Musset?[33] What a work! I defy you to write one like that.

I recommend you to go into the lobby of Nadar the photographer's (*near Old England*). There you will see a lifesize photograph of Alexandre Dumas, and alongside it a terra-cotta bust of the same Dumas. He's supposed to be bringing out prefaces to *Manon Lescaut* and *Paul et Virginie*! And to think he has no idea how ridiculous he is!

Have you heard from Mme Sand? She doesn't write to me any more.

I embrace you.

> Your old
>
> G. Flaubert

Croisset
Thursday 8 [October 1874]

My dear old man,

Thank you for what you sent me. That's the attentiveness of a friend. 'I know you by it Marguerite.'[34] Thank Mr Lindau on my behalf, he is very kind. When my niece is here in about a week's time, I'll get her to translate his articles.[35]

As far as *Salammbô* is concerned, it would be as well to warn Mr Lindau and his publisher that this book was translated into German as soon as it came out, by Mme? (I've forgotten her name). It's a friend of Mme Cornu, the wife of a teacher at Jena I think; and I can't find the book, it has a yellow cover.

If there were to be a few shekels to be made on that front, I should be glad. I leave it all up to you.

I'm waiting to hear from the Cluny before leaving Croisset.

Bouvard and Pécuchet have just arrived at their house in the country; I shall have finished the first chapter at the end of next week. These theatrical matters, which I don't really care about, will be a disruption, but I shall come back here as soon as I can.

In the meantime, I embrace you.

G. Flaubert

Are you enjoying the internecine feuds among the Bonapartists, the quarrels between the Jéromists and the Louloushians?[36] Could it be funnier?

I feel a real need to write a play about Bazaine's escape.[37] But all sense of the comic is dead. In former times that story would have had people in fits of laughter. It has passed almost unnoticed. Oh Barbarians! As M. de Voltaire used to say.

[Paris]
Wednesday 3 o'clock [25 November 1874]

What's the matter then? Are you more ill? Why aren't I seeing you? Why haven't I heard from you?

Zola and Daudet want to reorganise our banquets. But we need our great Turgenev for that.

I've taken *The Weaker Sex* away from the Cluny, and it's now with the Gymnase. I'm waiting to hear from Montigny.[38]

Let me know what you're up to.

Your
G. Flaubert

[Paris]
[Winter/Spring 1875]³⁹[39]

My dear friend,
    Tomorrow I dine, I think, at Mme Commanville's. Come and collect me there at 9 o'clock, and we'll go to old father Hugo's. Answer this, so that I shall know whether to wait for you or not. No! Don't bother. I'll wait for you until half past nine.

Your
G. Flaubert

[Paris]
Saturday evening 9 o'clock [3 April 1875]

My dear friend,
    You can no longer hope to be considered a *quiet old gentleman*, but rather a *young scatterbrain*. For you promised to send me this morning a line from your illustrious pen to let me know whether Monday's dinner is on. Daudet has been waiting for an answer from me since Wednesday. Can you come to our fraternal feasting the day after tomorrow? And should I count on you tomorrow?

Your old
G. Flaubert

If you honour my salon with your presence tomorrow, I shall introduce you to somebody famous and *funny*. Yesterday I read *Flamarande* and *The Two Brothers*.[40] I'm terribly disappointed with them.

Paris
[Monday 12 April 1875]

It's tomorrow at a quarter past nine, at 3 quai Voltaire, at M. Leloir the painter's. It's in a studio at the top of the house, top floor.
    Come any way, I've seen the rehearsal. It'll be superb. You'll enjoy it a lot.[41]
    Until tomorrow.

Your
G. Flaubert

Croisset
Saturday 3 July [1875]

I'm upset to hear that you're ill, my good dear old fellow. As for me, things aren't going at all well! Not at all! *B. and P.* have got stuck. I have embarked on an absurd enterprise, I realise it now, and I'm afraid of getting no further. I think I'm *drained*.

And then to tell you the truth, I have at the moment the greatest anxieties (in my personal life), money worries of the most serious kind. My poor head aches as if someone had been beating me with a stick. The present is no joke and the future scares me.

As I am incapable of all work, it's possible that towards the middle of August I shall go to Concarneau for two months with G. Pouchet.[42] I shall go fishing and eat lobster.

I could do with sleeping for a year. I'm harassed out of existence. There's the truth.

As soon as you're at Bougival, drop me a line to let me know how you withstood the journey.

My niece, who is at my side, sends you her greetings.
Your old
Gve Flaubert embraces you.

[Croisset]
July 30 [1875]

My last letter was 'lugubrious' according to you, dear friend. But I have reason to be lugubrious, for I must tell you the truth: my nephew Commanville is *absolutely* ruined. And I'm going to be seriously affected by it.

What makes me despair in all this, is the position of my poor niece. My (paternal) heart is suffering cruelly. Some very sad days are beginning: lack of money, humiliation, our lives turned upside down. This is the end, and my brain has been annihilated. I no longer feel capable of anything at all. I shan't get over it, my dear friend. It has cut me to the quick.

What days we spend! As I really don't want to inflict them on you, I put off until later the visit you promised me in yesterday's letter. We can't receive you at the moment. And God knows if a hug from my old Turgenev wouldn't relieve the strain on my heart!

I don't know yet if I shall go to Concarneau. In any case, it won't be for a month or six weeks.

I haven't written to Mme Sand for a very long time. Well tell her that I'm thinking of her more than ever. But I haven't got the strength to write to her.

We're going to have to salvage what we can. It'll be a long business. What shall we have left? Not a lot. That's the only certainty. I hope none the less to be able to keep Croisset. But the good times are over, and I see only a wretched old age before me. The most convenient thing for me would be if I were to die.

I'm such an egoist that I haven't said anything about you! I realise it. Why haven't I got your problems? And I don't wish mine on anybody.

Send me your news and always love your

G. Flaubert

Croisset
Tuesday evening [10 August 1875]

No, my good old fellow, don't come. It would be too sad for you and for me.

Please tell Mme Sand all you know. The situation is completely without hope for the moment, and the future doesn't look any better. It has been a *mortal blow*. It remains to be seen how long it will take me to die from it.

I embrace you with all the strength I have left.

Your
G. Flaubert

[Croisset]
Sunday [12 September 1875]

Don't be cross with me, my dear fellow, if I've been such an age without writing to you. My life is so awful that I am physically crushed.

Tomorrow I am leaving for Deauville, where I shall sell my last bit of land. Thanks to that, the bankruptcy of my nephew will, I think, be avoided. Then at the end of the week I'll be at Concarneau; and from there I'll send you my news.

I'm thinking of you and I embrace you.

Your old
G. Flaubert

III
October 1875–Spring 1878

After the financial disaster of his nephew Ernest Commanville's bankruptcy, Flaubert went on holiday with an old Rouen friend to Concarneau, a Breton fishing port, in the hope of calming his agitated nerves. Feeling so demoralised that he was unable to work on his major literary project *Bouvard and Pécuchet*, he undertook a much smaller scale work, three short stories. Turgenev became quite intimately involved with these poetic pieces of Flaubert, translating two of them for inclusion in a Russian journal, in an attempt to return a little solvency to his friend's financial affairs. On his own account, he completed *Virgin Soil*, having laboured on it for four years, during a summer spent on his estate at Spasskoye in 1876. The book was published the following spring, and its author had to face hostility and adverse reviews, just as Flaubert had had to with *Sentimental Education* some years earlier.

Turgenev's financial affairs also suffered that year, as a result of the Russo-Turkish War of 1877, which led to a devaluation of the ruble. In France, too, this was a time of political upheaval; the events known as the crisis of 16 May only served to damn further President Macmahon in the eyes of Flaubert and Turgenev. He dismissed the prime minister, hoping that his nominee, the Duc de Broglie, a supporter of the Orleanist branch of the royal family, would obtain a majority vote. When his plan failed, he simply dissolved the chamber and called an election. Although he sought to manipulate the electoral process, his royalist majority was greatly reduced, yet he managed to hold on to the presidential office until the beginning of 1879.

Turgenev was suffering from renewed attacks of gout at this time, and so all in all, the two novelists saw little during these years to relieve the pessimism that was already a determining factor in their world view.

Hotel Sergent Concarneau (Finistère)
Sunday 3 October [1875]

How are you my great Turgenev? And how are those around you?

As for me, I have calmed down a bit. That's not to say I'm cheerful, but my grief is less acute; and as the bankruptcy of my poor nephew has been definitively avoided, the pangs of anguish have lessened. It remains to be seen how we shall live now, and if I shall be able to salvage anything from the wreckage of my fortune. In spite of all efforts at reasoning and all the resolutions I want to make, I feel that I'm finished, my good friend! I've received a violent blow on the head which has smashed my brain, there's the truth of it.

I have abandoned *B and P.*, with which I was making no headway (will I take it up again later? Problematical); and so as to have something to occupy myself with, I'm going to try and write a little short story, a legend that figures in the stained-glass windows of Rouen Cathedral. It'll be very short, thirty-odd pages at most. The prospect doesn't really fill me with delight, but it's in order to keep busy and to see if I can still put a sentence together – which I doubt.

I get up at 9 o'clock, I stuff myself with lobster, I have a nap on my bed, I walk along the seashore, I go to bed at ten o'clock. I'm reading nothing. I'm living like an oyster. From time to time, my companion Georges Pouchet dissects a fish or a mollusc in front of me. And that's all. And I think about the past, about my childhood, my youth, all that which will never return. I indulge in boundless melancholy; and the next day, it starts all over again. When one's thoughts no longer naturally turn to the future, one is an old man. That's the stage I'm at.

In other times, this country would have delighted me. But the spectacle of nature is not so good for agitated souls as people say. It only confirms you in the conviction of your own nothingness and impotence.

I realise that this is not a very lively letter. Never mind, it will prove to you that I'm thinking about you.

How is your health? And the gout? You should be back in Paris now? Write me a long letter. You will give me much pleasure.

I embrace you.

Your old wreck
G. Flaubert

Les Frenes Bougival
Monday 11 October 75

The sight of your handwriting, my good old Flaubert gave me the greatest pleasure – and reading your letter even more so: you're surfacing again – and you're making – I was going to say literary plans!! Anyway, you are pleased at the thought that you are going to work. That's good – and I'm sure that you'll give us *thirty* pages.

Les Frenes
Friday 18 October 75

I had got thus far with my letter, my good friend, when something came along to interrupt me – and now, to my great surprise, I've just come across it in my blotter. I thought it had been sent long ago. I feel very foolish and I take up where I left off.

I was saying that I am very pleased at the idea of the *thirty* pages. I also have just promised my Russian publisher a story of 30 pages (2 printer's sheets) for *26* November – final deadline! And I still haven't even thought of the first word. My big novel has been put off more or less indefinitely – even more so than B. and P. – my publisher is screaming out for something from me! And so I've committed myself. Let's see which of us will finish first.

Alas yes! We are both old – my good friend; it's undeniable, let us at least try to enjoy life as old men do. By the way – have you read in the 'République Française' (of the 10th and 11th) a serial entitled 'A Child's Suicide' – and signed X? It made a strong impression on me. The man who wrote it evidently belongs to your school; if he is young – he shows promise. Try to get hold of the thing and give me your opinion.

Here all are well. I have had quite a violent attack of cystitis – I think that's what it's called, inflammation of the bladder; I spent two dreadful nights, I stayed in my bed for three days; at last it has more or less cleared up. These little 'mementoes' are the visiting cards that Madam Death sends us, so that we shan't forget her.

We are staying here until 1 November; the weather is mild, grey and damp – not unpleasant. I shall not be able to live in my new house this year[1] – but I come here from time to time, I write my letters here, like this one for example. There's a good fire in the hearth – and yet I feel cold in the back.

There has also been a nice little serial by Mme Sand in 'Le Temps' (written in 1829! – when she was 25) – you must have read it. Zola has written a magnificent article on the Goncourts in his Russian magazine. That will get their novels translated.

Let me know the – probable – date of your return to Croisset. I imagine you won't stay much longer at the seaside, and you'll come to Paris, in spite of everything. Your friends plan to gather round you, to keep you warm.

In the meantime give my regards to Mme Commanville. As for you, I embrace you – and I am

Your old faithful
Iv. Turgenev

[Concarneau]
Thursday [21 October 1875]

Damn it all! Youwill have finished your thirty pages before I've got to my tenth. For in spite of my resolutions and incomparable efforts of will, I'm hardly making any progress at all. I have relapses of depression, my good old fellow, bouts of tiredness, where I feel that I'm going to die. It's indigestion from all the cups of bitterness I've had to swallow these last six months. Ah and I've had some! I've had some! As for the future, I don't want to think about it any more (but I do). Perhaps it will be less bad than I think? In any case, one does not recover when one is so far gone; and deep down I am really ill. I hope to maintain some standards, that is, not to be a burden to others; but that's all.

I read on your recommendation *A Child's Suicide.* I don't know what to think about it. Obviously it's powerful stuff, but the *writing* of it is very inadequate. Although it's full of vigorous brush strokes, I find that the characters don't come across clearly. The hero, the suicide victim, is too grotesque. The author has forgotten an essential point, namely the fear a corpse inspires in children. All of this doesn't prevent this little work from being very remarkable. It's like a piece of Zola.

In my moments of idleness, and they are many (for as it rains frequently I have to spend whole days at a time in my hotel room, sitting by my fire), I'm reading Saint-Simon and rereading M. de Voltaire's short stories, then *Le Siècle* and *Le Temps* and *Le Phare de la Loire*; for here they are radical free-thinkers. I watch my companion dissect fish. All this helps to pass the time, but it doesn't fill my heart with delirious happiness. Ah, how a bit of happiness would do me good!

There are some consolations however. The other day, at Quimper, a citizen of Brest was condemned to hard labour for having raped his three daughters and his sixteen-year-old son. What a constitution! You and I couldn't give such evidence of a robust state of health!

I shall return to Paris directly from here in the first week of November.

My niece is installed in our new lodgings (for I shall live with her now), 240 rue du Faubourg-Saint-Honoré.

So I'll see you soon, my very dear old fellow.
                    Your
                    G.F. who embraces you.

[Paris]
Tuesday evening [2 May 1876]

Oh! I'm not a prude! I don't have to be asked twice: I accept. So until Friday between half past 6 and 7, I shall be ready, my good dear fellow.

Why didn't you come on Sunday? Our winter is drawing to an end. We must see each other more often.

At the Salon there are two or three highly praised pictures that I find exasperating. We'll talk about them.

ı think that Jeokhanan (translate: Saint John the Baptist) will come. But I must finish my old woman, and I'm barely a third of the way.[2]

Farewell. Until Friday.

Your
G. Flaubert

[Paris]
[20 May 1876]

Mme Brainne,[3] 141 avenue Malakoff (porte Maillot) on the first floor above the mezzanine, today Saturday at seven o'clock precisely.

But, oh you absentminded creature, I wrote all that down for you myself last Sunday in your notebook.

Your
G. Flaubert

I spent the night reading Renan's new book, which delighted me.[4]

Spasskoye Mtsensk Province of Oryol
Sunday 18 June 1876

My dear friend,
Since this morning, I have been at my Patmos – and it has the effect of a wet blanket. (Have you noticed that it's generally at such times that one writes to one's best friends?) The temperature is 32 degrees Réaumur in the shade – and added to that – thanks to a frost of minus 9 degrees below zero on 21 May – all the greenery in the garden is streaked with little dead leaves that make me think vaguely of the corpses of small children – and my old lime trees give only a thin and sparse shade that is pitiful to see. Add to that the fact that my brother who was supposed to be waiting for me here to arrange some money matters that are very important to me, left for Carlsbad five days ago, that I think I'm going to have an attack of gout (which happened to me

at the same time and in the same place two years ago); that I have almost certain proof that my bailiff is robbing me – and that I shan't be able to get rid of him – you see the situation! The death of Mme Sand has also distressed me greatly, very greatly.[5] I know that you went to Nohant for the funeral, and I wanted to send a telegramme of condolence in the name of the Russian reading public, but a sort of ridiculous modesty held me back, through fear of the *Figaro* and of the publicity – stupid things, all in all! The Russian readership is amongst those on which Mme Sand has had the greatest influence – and it needed to be said, by God – and I didn't have the right – after all. But there you are!!

Poor dear Mme Sand! She loved us both – you especially – that was only natural. What a heart of gold she had! Such an absence of all low, petty or false sentiments – what a good fellow she was and what a fine woman! And now all of that is there, in the horrible relentless hole in the ground, silent, stupid – and it doesn't even know what it is it's devouring!

Come – there's nothing to be done about it and let us try to keep our chins above water.

I'm writing to you at Croisset – I assume you are there – have you got back down to work? If I do nothing here – that must mean it's all up with me. There is a silence here, which you can't possibly imagine; not a single neighbour in a radius of twenty kilometres – everything languishes, is motionless! The house is wretched – but not too hot – and the furniture is good. A writing desk – fine – and an armchair with a double rush seat! And for example, there is a dangerous sofa, as soon as one is on it, one falls asleep. I shall try to avoid it. I shall start by finishing St Julian.

Before me in a corner of the room there is an old Byzantine icon, all blackened, in a silver frame, nothing but a huge stiff and gloomy face – it troubles me rather – but I can't have it taken down, my manservant would take me for a pagan, and here that's no joking matter.

Send me a couple of lines more cheerful than these.

I embrace you and am your old friend

Iv. Turgenev

P.S.   Did you know that the Circassian Hassan who is killing off ministers in pairs, like partridges, inspires a certain respect in me?[6]
P.S.   Friendly greetings to your niece and her husband.

Croisset
Sunday evening 25 June 1876

How I seized upon your letter yesterday, my dear old man, as soon as I recognised your handwriting! For I was starting to miss you badly! So having embraced, let us talk.

I am distressed to hear that you have money problems and fears for your health. Let us hope that you are wrong and that the gout will leave you alone.

The death of poor old mother Sand caused me infinite pain. I blubbered shamelessly at her funeral, and that twice over: the first time on kissing her granddaughter Aurore (whose eyes were so much like hers that day, that it seemed almost like a reincarnation) and the second as her coffin passed in front of me. There was some scandal of course! So as not to offend 'public opinion', its eternal, execrable voice, they carried her off to the church. I must tell you all the details of this contemptible action. My heart was heavy and I could positively have murdered M. Adrien Marx.[7] The very sight of him took away all my appetite for dinner that evening at Châteauroux. Oh what a tyrant the *Figaro* is! What a public pestilence. I suffocate with rage whenever I think about those fools.

My companions on the journey, Renan and the Prince Napoleon,[8] were charming, the former perfect in his tact and respect, and he saw through it all from the beginning better than either of us.

You are right to regret the loss of our friend, for she loved you dearly and never spoke of you without calling you 'good Turgenev'. But why pity her? She lacked nothing and will remain a great figure.

The good country people wept a great deal round her grave. We were up to our ankles in mud in that little country cemetery. A gentle rain was falling. Her funeral was like a chapter from one of her books.

Forty-eight hours later, I was back at my Croisset, where *I am amazingly glad to be*. I enjoy the greenness, the trees and the silence in quite a new way. I have taken up cold-water treatment (ferocious hydrotherapy) again and I'm working like a madman.

My *Story of a Simple Soul* will doubtless be finished towards the end of August. After that I shall embark on *Hérodias*! But how difficult it is! By God it's difficult! The further I get, the more aware of it I become. It seems to me that French prose can achieve a *beauty* that we can't even imagine. Don't you find that our friends don't care over much for Beauty? And yet it is the most important thing in the world!

And what about you? Are you working? Is *St Julian* coming on? What I'm going to say is silly, but I really *want to see* it printed in Russian! Besides the fact that a translation by you 'tickles the proud weakness of my heart', the only resemblance between Agamemnon and me.

When you left Paris, you hadn't read Renan's new book.[9] It seems charming to me. 'Charming' is the right word. Do you share my opinion? However, I have no idea what has been happening in the world for the last two weeks, not once having read a single newspaper. Fromentin sent me his book on 'old masters'.[10] As I know very little about Dutch painting, it doesn't have the same interest for me as it will for you. It's clever, but too long, too long! The said Fromentin seems to me to be greatly influenced by Taine. Ah! I was forgetting! The poet Mallarmé[11] (the author of *The Faun*) made me a present of a book he is editing: *Vathek*, an oriental story, written in French by an Englishman at the end of the last century. It's curious.

I drift off into dreams (and desires) when I think that this sheet of paper will go to you in your house that I shall never know! And I'm cross that I don't have a more precise idea of your surroundings.

If you're hot where you are, we are not exactly suffering from cold here either. I spend the whole day behind closed shutters, in exclusive solitude. At mealtimes, I have for distraction the sight of my faithful Emile and my greyhound.

My niece, to whom I shall convey your greetings, is going off at the end of the month to Eaux-Bonnes with her husband, and I shan't leave here until the end of September, when I go to Daudet's first night. But by then you will have been back at Les Frenes for some time.

You'll be pleased to learn that my nephew's affairs seem to have taken a turn for the better. At least there is some blue sky on the horizon.

Yes my dear old fellow, let us try, in spite of everything, to keep our [heads] above water. Look after yourself, work well and come back soon.

I embrace you tenderly and vigorously.

Your
G. Flaubert

Write to me, won't you?

Spasskoye Mtsensk Province of Oryol
Tuesday 4 July 1876

My dear old fellow,
I am writing from here to you at Croisset – from one Patmos to another. I received your letter yesterday and, you see, I reply without delay.

Yes, the life of Mme Sand was a full one, and yet when speaking of her, you say *poor* old mother Sand – this adjective is fitting for the dead, for after all, they are to be pitied, death being such a hideous thing. I remember little Aurore's eyes: there is an amazing depth and goodness about them, and they are indeed like her grandmother's.

They are almost too full of goodness for a child's eyes. It seems that Zola has written a long article on Mme Sand in his Russian magazine. It is a fine article, but rather hard, they say. Zola can't make a complete judgement on Mme S. There is too much distance between them.

I can just see you rolling your eyes in anger at M. Adrien Marx. Such fungi flourish in a particular kind of mire.

You are working at Croisset . . . Well, I'm going to surprise you. Never before have I worked as I have done since I've been here. I stay up all night, bent over my desk. I have new faith in the illusion that it is possible to say things – not that no one has ever said before (I don't care about that) but to say them differently! And yet I am weighed down with problems – money maters, administrative affairs, tenancies and I don't know what else! (On this subject I can tell you that all is not as bad as I believed at first – and by the way I am delighted to hear that there is a bit of blue sky in your nephew's affairs.) But St Julian is being neglected because of this frenetic activity. My damned novel has taken hold of me in an all-consuming way. In spite of everything though, he reassured: the translation is already promised for the October issue of the *European Messenger*. It will be in it, unless I die before then.

I haven't read the articles by Fromentin, nor have I read Renan's book. I can't read anything at the moment, unless it's the newspaper I get here, that tells of trouble in the East and makes me wonder.[12] I think it's the beginning of the end! But how many severed heads, women, girls and children raped and disembowelled will there be before then! I don't think we (I mean the Russians) will be able to avoid war.

You want to know what my house looks like? It's quite ugly. Here is something approximating to it:

I don't know if you can work it out from this: it's a wooden house, very old and clad with planks distempered in pale lilac; there is a verandah in front with climbing ivy; the two roofs (a and b) are of corrugated iron painted *green*; the top part is uninhabitable and the windows are nailed up. This little house is all that remains of a vast horseshoe-shaped dwelling – like this:

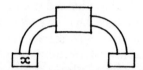

that was burnt down in 1840; x marks the part that I live in. Last evening, with your letter in my pocket, I was sitting on the steps of my verandah with 60-odd peasant women before me, nearly all dressed in red and very ugly (all except one, a young bride of *16*, who had just had a fever and who looks like the Virgin of St Sixtus in Dresden), they were dancing like bears and marmots, and singing with voices that were hard and rasping, but in tune. It was a little celebration that they had asked me to organise – nothing simpler: two buckets of brandy, cakes, hazelnuts and there you are. They were jigging about, I watched them at it and felt horribly sad.

The little Virgin of St Sixtus is called Mary as is fitting.
That's enough. I shall write to you again before I leave.
In the meantime, I embrace you affectionately.

Your old
I. Turgenev

P.S.   I find the colour of the landscape very muted here – the sky, the vegetation, the earth – a quite warm and golden pallor; it would be no more than pretty, were it not that the bold outlines, the great uniform spaces, contribute an element of grandeur.

Les Frenes Bougival
Tuesday 8 August 76

(N.B. It's by chance that I'm writing on this dandified paper.)[13]

My dear friend, I arrived here two days ago, after a hectic journey across Russia, Germany etc. Your letter gave me great pleasure – you are well and you are working. I also am well and I have been working –

for unbelievably! – I have *finished* my great devil of a novel – and I'm going to set to work again, for it has to be copied out, and it must be ready in two months, which won't be easy, you know what copying is like. There are some pages without a single line left on them. I've seen many things and many people, like Ulysses, and I returned to find all my little world here in good health. I showed the door to my bailiff who has robbed me of something like 130,000 francs, quite a considerable portion of my fortune. Why was I so stupid? Through laziness I let things deteriorate to a situation of blind trust, although I felt (is that the right grammatical form?) strongly, looking at that sickly sweet bearded face, that it belonged to a rogue. Anyway, never mind! Let him have my money!

I fully intend to drag myself away from my copying for 2 or 3 days (towards the 25th of this month) to go to Croisset to hear you read the 'Parrot'.[14] Alongside my copying, I shall finish the translation of St Julian, for it's supposed to come out in Russia on 1 November.

I've just read that man's article on Renan. It's unworthy. All this *République des Lettres* stinks of affectation and I don't know what else that's false and low.

Zola has written to me. He is well and is returning to Paris in mid-September.

I like my chalet; I shall like it even better when it has lost its smell of newness. The weather is too fine. The greenness of the trees in front of my window has a golden velvety splendour. It's very pretty.

When you write to your niece, remember me to her. And I shall see you in a little more than two weeks' time.

Your old
Iv. Turgenev

[Croisset]
Thursday [17 August 1876]

Well, I too have *finished*!!! And at the moment I am copying it out, which isn't a very big task, as the work is short.

So, my good dear old fellow, YOU MUST come and hear it as soon as possible; and if the thing pleases you, it would yet again please me if it were to appear in a Russian journal, in order to make a bit of money. (Whether it's more or less well translated doesn't really bother me!) Anyway, we'll talk about all that. In not more than a week's time, won't it be? I await your visit like parched earth. What heat, devil take it!

It seems to me that we have a lot of things to say to each other.

In two or three [days] I expect a note from you saying: 'I'm coming'.

Greetings to all the rest, and a big hug from your

G. Flaubert

The Chalet Les Frenes Bougival
Wednesday 23 August 76

My dear friend,
I didn't write back to you straightaway, because I wanted to be able to fix definitely the date of my arrival at Croisset – and it wasn't easy – but I've just received your telegramme – and I see I must tell you that I *can't* come before *10 September*, but then *for certain*. I'm delighted that you've finished your work – if I find that *to start with* it's better for St Julian to come out in a *Russian* Review – I'll set about the task, although the other is just about finished. You know we still have some leeway before 1 November.

I'm snowed under with copying – and that's a job that bores me.

Otherwise I am well, but I feel myself enveloped in a fog of old age, which is very unpleasant.

So, my friend – until the 10th without fail!
I embrace you.

Your
Iv. Turgenev

[Croisset]
Thursday evening 24 [August 1876]
Anniversary of the massacre of St Bartholomew's Eve

My good dear old fellow
I shan't expect you on the 10th as I shan't be at Croisset then. But if you would like to put off your visit for a week, with what joy I shall receive it! I have to make a trip away, or rather two or three little ones, one of which is to Saint-Gratien.

But I cannot accept, my dear friend, that you should be my sworn translator from now on. Once is a great honour; but to commit the offence a second time would distress me. There is no shortage of people in Russia who can translate me after a fashion, witness those who are translating Zola's correspondence. We'll talk about it.

I'll see you soon. I embrace you.

Your old
G. Flaubert

I'll write to tell you where I am.

[Paris]
Wednesday [September 1876]

My good old fellow,
Can you be in the galerie de l'Horloge in the Opéra Arcade next Friday at 7 o'clock? (The said galerie de l'Horloge is the one where the public conveniences are!)
I shall be at home at 3 o'clock, on my way back from Saint-Gratien. I shall make two or three calls. I shall go and take a bath in the rue Saint-Arnoud. Then I shall have myself 'done up' at Goubert's, the Opéra hairdresser. After which we'll dine and spend the evening together. It's agreed, isn't it?

All the best
G. Flaubert

[Paris]
[Saturday 9 September 1876]

My dear friend,
Can we count on you? We fear you may be ill. In any case (and on account of Charpentier) our dinner will be tomorrow: we're meeting at my place at half past 4 to listen to *A Simple Soul*. After which we shall go to the restaurant at the *Opéra-Comique*. Try to come.

Your
G. Flaubert

You'll be receiving an invitation to dine next Wednesday from Princess Mathilde.
I was very sorry not to see you yesterday.

[Paris]
Wednesday 5 o'clock [13 September 1876]

My dear friend,
Daudet confided to me yesterday that his first night[15] won't now be until Monday, although it has been announced for Saturday. It's on Saturday a 1 o'clock that they're holding the dress rehearsal. If you want to come, you need only give your name: I shall be at the theatre at 1 o'clock precisely. *Please* let us have a note to let us know whether to expect you.
I shall be free from Monday morning onwards, and on Tuesday we

shall head off together towards my native land. The five to one express seems to me the most convenient.

Try to come to the Vaudeville on Saturday, where we'll make arrangements for Monday.

Your old fellow who embraces you

G. Flaubert

[Paris]
Thursday 2 o'clock [14 September 1876]

Agreed! Until *Tuesday*. Don't let me down, else I die. Awaiting this great pleasure, my poor old fellow, I embrace you.

G. Flaubert

The Chalet Les Frenes Bougival
Sunday 23 September 76

My ferocious old fellow!

I got back here without mishap; I have not had time to see Magny, but I've seen Pellé. I put the contentious question to him and he replied: 'It is done, and often – but it is not in the rules of good *cuisine!*'

The result of this is that I owe you 6 bottles of champagne; but if I don't have the *material* victory, I have the *moral* one!!

I have gone back to my copying – this evening I shall reread 'A Simple Soul' for the second time.

A thousand friendly greetings to all at Croisset – I hope your niece will soon be better – and I embrace you.

He who eats *hot* roast chicken without mustard.

I.T.

[Croisset]
Wednesday [27 September 1876]

Oh Stubborn Man,

Well? Are you sufficiently . . . But no! I wish to indulge you with my clemency.

Don't you think we could have spent our last hour talking about something else? But you stuck at it and kept coming back to it. Anyway, let's say no more about it. That's another hour you *owe* me, you creature of passage, whom it's impossible to keep under one's roof.

Nothing new since your departure. My niece is still laid up on her sofa. The rain is falling, and I have just finished my notes on Flavius Josephus, who was a fine bourgeois. There you are.

This story *Hérodias* scares me stiff. The plan is becoming a little clearer, but only a [little].

I received a letter from Raoul-Duval this morning, who thinks you are still here (ah yes!) and he begs to be remembered to you.

Don't trouble yourself with translating *A Simple Soul*. Find someone else for the job, which I'm embarrassed to see you doing (although really very flattered).

When will you come back now? When shall we see each other again? Keep cheerful and think of me sometimes.

Your old fellow who embraces you

G. Flaubert

The Chalet Les Frenes Bougival (Seine-et-Oise)
Wednesday 25 October 76

I'm writing to you on a Wednesday – and your letter is dated a Wednesday – but how many weeks have gone by? Two, three, a hundred, a thousand – I can't tell! What have I done in all this time? Nothing and I know nothing about it. The days have fled by like running water, like sand. What about you, have you been working? How is Mme Commanville? She has been up and about for ages I hope. When are you coming to Paris? We are staying here for another ten days. The sky has been grey all this time. I have read nothing. Ah yes I have! I read the second Canto of 'Don Juan' by Lord Byron – that was a ray of sunlight through all this greyness.

We have had two or three evenings of fine music.

One night I had an attack of renal colic. I thought I was going to die. And that's all!

Drop me a line and give my regards to M. and Mme Commanville. I feel dazed, but that doesn't prevent me from embracing you.

Your

Iv. Turgenev

Croisset
Saturday [28 October 1876]

I was starting to get anxious about you, my very dear old fellow. I was afraid you were ill.

As for me, I'm working away. Except for twenty-four hours spent at Vaudreuil at Raoul–Duval's place, at the end of last week, I haven't moved from here since your departure. I've finished taking notes for *Hérodias*, and I'm working out my plan. For I have embarked on a work that's not easy, because of the explanations necessary for the French reader. To make such complex matters come across in a clear and lively manner is a gigantic task. But if there were no difficulties, where would the pleasure be?

Are you reading good old Zola's dramatic serial? I recommend last Sunday's to you as a curiosity. It seems to me that his theories are constricting and they end up getting on my nerves.

As far as success is concerned, I think he's scuppering himself with *L'Assommoir*. The reading public, which was coming round to him, will turn away and never return. That's where the mania for taking sides, for sticking to a system leads you. Let louts speak in loutish language, fine, but why should the author share their style? And he thinks it's ever so clever, without realising that by this very quirk, he's reducing the impact of the effect he seeks to create.

In order to get on more quickly, I feel I want to stay at Croisset for quite a while yet, until the New Year, perhaps until the end of January. That way I shall have perhaps finished by the end of February. For if I want to bring out a volume at the beginning of May, I shall have to finish *Hérodias* promptly, so that the translation could come out in Russia in April. What's happening about that for *A Simple Soul*? And *Saint Anthony*, when shall I see it?

My niece is back on her feet, and begs me, as does her husband, to send you their best wishes.

Young Guy de Maupassant has published an article on me in the *République des Lettres* that makes me blush. It's really the work of a fanatical devotee, but there is a nice line about the two of us at the end.[16]

We'll give you a performance of the infamous play this winter.[17] And he's working on another one – even stronger stuff: men only in this one!

What else have I to tell you? Nothing if not that I love you, my dear great man, but you know that already.

I embrace you.

Your old

G. Flaubert

How is your nephritis? Is it linked to your gout? Or is it yet another delight? I think not? Look after yourself.

I hope to start writing in about a week. At present I'm dreadfully scared, a fear such as to make one have novenas said for the success of the thing!

Les Frenes Bougival
Wednesday 8 November 76

My dear friend,

I am going through all the agonies of packing – we're going to Paris the day after tomorrow; once we're settled in there – I'll write you a longer letter.

'The European Messenger' has let me know that they can't put in St Julian *under* my name *before* my novel, given that I promised not to publish anything by me or signed by me before that thing. But as the novel will be included in the January issue, St Julian will be in February's – before its publication in France.

I think I've found a good translator for *A Simple Soul*.

I'm delighted that Mme Commanville is better. Give her my regards.

As for the gigantic difficulties of 'Herodiade' [*sic*] – I *believe* you – but I'm sure you'll overcome them in the end.

I haven't read Zola's serial – but I've read the first part of 'L' Assommoir'. Good God!   We'll talk about it.

I shall write to you in two or three days' time, as soon as I'm settled in Paris.

My renal colic was just an isolated incident, but a very disagreeable one at that – since then I've not been too bad.

Until the next time. I embrace you.

Your
I. Turgenev

50 rue de Douai Paris
Saturday 2 December 76
Saturday 9 December 76

My dear fellow,

Just a week ago, I picked up this sheet of paper to write to you; and I didn't write a word. I am in a poor state of mine; I feel old, grey, dull, useless – and stupid. I've had an attack of gout, but even that came to nothing. I'm correcting the proofs of my novel that have been sent to me from St Petersburg and I find it flat and insignificant. I see hardly anybody. I think you stay away from Paris for far too long. If I'd been able to have a chat with you, all this would have sorted itself out – but it would take too long to put it all down on paper and a) it's tiring and b) when writing one has to say *everything* – even self-evident truths. We had a dinner with Zola and Goncourt; Daudet couldn't come. We missed you. M. Pellé gave us an awful dinner; we mustn't go back there. Come now – when shall we see you in Paris? Is your work coming on? How is your health? Goncourt read us an extract from his novel,[18] his voice was tremulous with emotion. It seemed to me strange to see a grey-haired man feeling such emotion. What he read seemed good, but a bit too sketchy. I've dipped into *L'Assommoir*. I'm not very taken with it (this strictly between the two of us). There is skill in it – but it's heavy going – and there is too much stirring of chamber pots in it.

Now then, when are you coming back? Let me know without delay, don't be like me.

And what do you say to the fine mess that we're all floundering in here at the moment?

There will most certainly be a war[19] whatever 'they' say. I hope to have an income of 10,000 rubles (for the year 1877). In good times, that would be 35,000 francs. In mediocre times 30,000 and in bad times 25,000. And I can only count on 25,000, no more. As I shall have 10,000 francs worth of bills and as much in debts, there won't be much left over. Patience!

Give my kindest regards to your niece and her husband. I am like a soft, ripe pear – an old rag – but I love you dearly and embrace you.

When shall we meet?

I. Turgenev

[Croisset]
Thursday 14 December [1876]

I didn't know what to think about your silence, my dear old fellow! And I had begged my niece (who has been in Paris for some time) to go and see if *my* Turgenev were not dead.

You seem sad and debilitated. Why? Is it the money problem? What about me then! I'm not working any the less for that though, and in fact more than ever. If I continue at this pace, I shall have finished *Hérodias* at the end of February. By New Year's Day I hope to be half-way. How will it turn out? I don't know. In any case it is taking on the appearance of a shouting match. For in fact there is nothing but shouting in it: Balling, Bombast, Hyperbole. Let's let our hair down!

Like you, I've read bits of *L'Assommoir*. I didn't like it. Zola is falling victim to inverted preciosity. He believes that there are vigorous words in the same way that Cathos and Madelon[20] believed that there were noble ones. He is getting carried away by his *System*. He has principles that are constricting his brain. Read his Monday serials and you'll see how he believes he has discovered 'Naturalism'! As for poetry and style, the two eternal elements, he never mentions them!

You can question our friend Goncourt on the same subject. If he's being honest he'll confess that French literature didn't exist before Balzac. That's where over-cleverness and the fear of falling into platitudes lead.

Have you read, in the December issue of Buloz's rag, an article by Renan that I find without equal in its originality and high moral tone?[21] Moreover, in the same issue, there is some gossip from that character Montégut, who, while denying any value to my books (to say nothing of *Salammbô*), compares me to Molière and Cervantes. I'm not modest but, although alone and 'in the privacy of the study', I blushed with shame. I can't imagine any more disgusting stupidity.

What's more, I read *no* newspapers. It was only last Sunday that I learnt, by chance, of the change of government, which I don't give a damn about anyway. As for the war, I wish: a) the total annihilation of Turkey, and b) that France be spared any consequences of the back-lash. Prussia's refusal to take part in the Exhibition seems to me pathetic. Base! Base!

N.B. – Now, my good man, give me a straight answer. Can my three stories be in print in Russian by next April? (*Hérodias* can be finished in February.) That way, I could bring them out in volume at the beginning of May. The destitution in which I find myself makes that *highly* desirable. Otherwise I'll have to put it off until the winter, and that would inconvenience me.

In order to get on more quickly, it is quite likely that I shall stay here until the end of January. But what celebrations there'll be when I'm with you again! I'm longing for it.

Come on, shake off your sloth! Write to me! I am virtuous and deserve special consideration.

Your
G.F. embraces you tenderly.

P.S.   What a story about his lordship Germiny, arrested for buggery![22] Such stories cheer one up and help to make life bearable.

50 rue de Douai Paris
Tuesday 19 December 76

My dear old man,

I've just got back from making a very virtuous family visit which took three days – and which was pretty boring. So here I am now answering your letter. Let's sort out the question of the three stories first.

St Julian is translated, and with the publisher – and will be paid for at my usual rate – i.e. you'll get 300 rubles (the ruble varies between 2 francs 85 centimes and 3 francs 30 centimes) per printer's sheet (16 pages). But there's the snag. I had to make a formal promise to my publisher and to the reading public (in a note that I was foolish enough to allow to be published) to let *nothing appear* under my name before my great devil of a novel. I have finished this novel, and I've sent it to St Petersburg, and it's being printed at this moment; only my publisher, who is as cunning as a snake, instead of printing it as a whole (which he promised categorically) is cutting it in half – so that it will come out in the two editions of 1–13 January and 1–13 February – and he has so succeeded in twisting me round his little finger (you know what a *soggy* pear I am) that I have agreed to this mutilation, which puts poor *Julian* off until 1–13 March. The two other stories would then have to be published in the 1–13 April edition; in any case, the *Simple Soul shouldn't appear on its own*. That would not be impossible according to what you say in your letter. I have given *A Simple Soul* to a Russian lady of letters who handles the language very well (she is here in Paris) – and if she does a creditable job, I could entrust Herodiade [*sic*] to her as well. Naturally I shall check the translation most carefully – I'll copy it out if necessary, for my name must be on it! Otherwise people will say: if he translated the first story, why didn't he translate the others? Are they less good then? We wouldn't get a good price that way. But – another hitch! I'm leaving for Petersburg (keep this to yourself) on *15 February* for a month. It's probable that you won't have finished by then, or if you have, I could only take the original, without having time to have a translation made; well, in that case, I'd have to find someone in Petersburg – which is not impossible. *Final Result*: try to finish Herodiade in the first few days of February. And then we'll see!

As for the other points dealt with in your letter, I'll reply very succinctly, because I don't want to go over the page:
(i)   Urgent request to hasten your return, because I miss you terribly.
(ii)   On the question of Zola – we're agreed. (N.B.   Friday is our dinner at the Opéra-Comique restaurant. Pellé is a swine.)
(iii) Renan. His article is very interesting – personally; but what a lack of colour and of life! I *see* nothing: neither Brittany, nor all his saints, nor his mother, nor his little girls who make his first love 'fragmented', nor himself! And why does he say that *God* gave him a daughter?
(iv) I haven't read M. Montégut, because he disgusts me.
There probably won't be a war; you are indirectly concerned, as it has a devil of an effect on the exchange rate against the ruble; the change of government leaves me indifferent. Germiny is enormous! It's enough to make one believe in a personal deity of irony and mockery!

I received a visit from Mme Commanville; I was very charmed and very flattered; I thought she looked splendidly well.

And now I embrace you.

Your

I.T.

[Croisset]

Sunday evening [24 December 1876]

Ouf! I have just completed a session of *ten hours at a stretch* hammering away at my work. So, for a breath of air, I shall be going shortly to midnight mass with the nuns at the Convent of Saint Barbara. See my good fellow! Can one be more romantic than that?

But this present communication (commercial style) is only to thank you in respect of the translations. Really, if I could get this volume out in the spring, after having published it as a serial (i) in Russia and (ii) in the Parisian journals, it would be a great help.

If you're only leaving at the end of February, everything will be ready, or very nearly so. In any case, there would still be time if it were 13 May (!), since I have the right, don't I, to publish elsewhere, and as I see fit, immediately afterwards. But if it's after that, it would mean waiting until winter.

What with such *phrenetic* work[23] (all the more as I haven't changed my ways) you can imagine that I shan't be in Paris before the end of January, or even the first few days of the following month.

Germiny continues to be a profound source of joy to me. Do you not savour all the sweetness of vengeance when such a thing befalls an 'hofficial gentleman'? Rays of heavenly glory mingling with the folds of the anus, judges robes hanging over the latrines. And the jeweller, what a gem! And the gnashing of teeth in the sacristy!   There's the subject for a play. Let's write it. You being out Elder, you must make Guy do it. I can feel it.

Thereupon I embrace you and wish you a Happy New Year. All the best.

Your old

G. Flaubert

50 rue de Douai Paris

2 January 77

My dear friend,

On the following page you'll find a piece of poetry dictated by a schoolmaster to his class (on the occasion of the New Year) which the son of our caretaker, a boy of 8 years, has just presented to his parents. The mother (who, by the way, cannot read) came to show his fine thing to Mme Viardot (she was so proud of it, she had tears in her eyes) and I hastened to copy out this pure masterpiece in order to send it to you. Sound the depths, if you can, of this school supervisor's soul, drowned in rhetoric.

I have an attack of gout in the knee; I hope it will be nothing – but for the moment I can't move.

And what about you, are you still working well? Is your health good?

I embrace you affectionately.

Iv. Turgenev

Dear Parents!
A new year begins its round
And you know what wishes in my heart are found.
There's one especially that in love we see:
To see you always loving me
As much as you I seek to please!
Jealous of lovers' joy
Time delights their bond to destroy.
This knot, once dear wearies them now,
And the wind carried away their vow.
And for the woman abandoned
More often the happy year
Is the one just ended!
But filial affection
Does not lead to rejection,
Always living, always the same,
Like to Vesta's temple's flame,
By time its progress is not halted,
Nor its passion ever extinguished.

[Croisset]
Thursday 3 o'clock [4 January 1877]

Thank you for your piece of poetry, my good Turgenev. It is *lovely*.

Look after your knee.

I'm working as much as I possibly can in order to be finished by 15 February – which looks like being difficult. What a lot of damned trouble I give myself.

Respects and greetings to all at your place.

Your
G.F. embraces you tenderly.

Croisset
Tuesday 16 January [1877]

My dear old fellow,

How is the gout? My niece wrote to me that you seemed morose. Is it as a result of your financial affairs? Goncourt told me that his are in a very bad way. And mine aren't taking a turn for the better either.

I wonder if it will be at all possible soon to live without bothering about money, without being a banker, or having to buy and sell things. A fine prospect for humanity: we shall all be grocers! The Greeks would never have achieved what they did without the mines of Laurium, which meant that they didn't have to earn a living. How philosophical one has to be, to bear to live, my dear friend!

I have worked in a Gargantuan fashion this winter. Thus my *Hérodias* is coming along. When I arrive in Paris (3 February, two weeks from next Saturday) I will have perhaps five or six pages to go. So I think I'll be able to give you it all (according to your instructions, Sir) towards 15 February. This way the volume would come out in French at the beginning or in the middle of May. There would still be time. But if you are leaving for Russia on the 15th we won't see you at all this winter? This doubt makes me uneasy.

I know Catulle has a play in rehearsal at the Ambigu.[24] If you see him, tell him I count on going to the first night.

What are they saying about *L'Assommoir*, out yesterday? I wrote to Zola not to send it to me. It would distract me, but I'm dying to read it.

I embrace you.

Your

G. Flaubert

50 rue de Douai Paris
Wednesday evening 24 January 1877

My dear old fellow,

I'm sending you two issues of 'Le Temps' where there is a little piece of silliness by me.[25] Read it when you have nothing better to do.

The first part of my novel[26] that has come out in Russia seems to be giving a lot of pleasure to my friends and very little to the reading public. The newspapers find me worn out and throw my own earlier works back in my face (like you with 'Madame Bovary').

I'm pleased to know you're working hard, and Mme Commanville, whom I've seen and found in good health and spirits, told me that you would come back sooner than you had supposed. Bravo! I have been missing you here. As for me, I shan't leave before early March.

Zola has sent me his 'L'Assommoir'. It's a thick volume, and I'm going to tackle it.

Poor Maupassant is losing every hair on his body! (He came to see me.) It's a stomach complaint, so he says. He is still as kind, but very ugly just now.

In spite of everything, I still believe that there will be a war in the spring.

And now I embrace you and say 'until we meet'.

Iv. Turgenev

[Croisset]
Wednesday evening 24 [January 1877]

My good dear old fellow,

You didn't tell me how long you are going to be in Russia. The idea that we shall have to leave each other as soon as we've met up is spoiling my winter for me in advance. It's annoying.

My niece wrote to me this morning to know *whom* I wanted to dinner on Sunday 4 February. I immediately replied: Turgenev.

And I shall have finished *Hérodias* before the 15th of next month!!! Perhaps even in a week's time. But I'm three parts dead from it.

I embrace you.

G. Flaubert

If you see our friends, let them know that I shall be at home on the afternoon of the 4th. That will save me the trouble of writing to them. I can't manage anything else.

Croisset
Friday, 2 o'clock [26 January 1877]

I cannot resist the need to tell you that your 'little piece of silliness' is a *masterpiece*! And I know what I'm talking about by God!

If that's a proof of decadence, as your compatriots make out, well be decadent!

How original and well-written it is! Not a single superfluous word! Such hidden strength! What masterly strokes. I'm delighted with it. All joking apart and without wishing to flatter, it seems to me first rate!

And I who begged Zola not to send me *L'Assommoir*, so as not to be distracted!!!

Farewell now! I'm counting on you for Sunday week!

Your old

G.F. embraces his old fellow.

At the top of the third column of the second issue, there is a dreadful sentence, on account of the many *thats*.

50 rue de Douai [Paris]
Wednesday 14 March [1877] 11.30 a.m.

My dear old fellow,

I've just written to Princess Mathilde that I shan't be able to go to her dinner; I'm terribly sorry, it's awfully bad luck, but I really can't show my face out of doors – I'm going out for the first time to go to a dentist and I'm coming straight back. I had violent neuralgia again last night.

I beg you to tell the princess that all this is unfortunately the truth.

Something else: Stasyulevich now writes that after due consideration he prefers to put the *two* legends together – in the 13 April edition. It's his business and perhaps he's right. I had written a little preface. That doesn't change anything for the publication here. Stasyulevich writes that as Hérodiade [*sic*] is the same length as St Julian he'll base his calculations on that – and will send the money straightaway (I gave him to understand in veiled terms that you would not be displeased!)

I shake your hand with melancholy.

Your

I. Turgenev

[Paris]
Wednesday 5 o'clock [14 March 1877]

Later on I shall paint a pathetic portrait of your condition to the princess. Send me a bulletin on your health tomorrow evening. It upsets me to know you're ill. As for the delay of a month, it doesn't bother me, except for the fear of a second delay. Tell them over there that it would have unfortunate consequences for me. I don't thank you for what you're doing for me, that would be an insult; and I embrace you.

G. Flaubert

[Paris]
Sunday morning [18 April 1877]

Yesterday at 5 o'clock, as I was going to change to come and call on you, Prince Napoleon came and paid me a visit. That's why you didn't see me.

Let me have news of you, poor dear old fellow. We missed you a lot at Taine's where there was a very pleasant little philosophical dinner. Try to be better for Wednesday.

Send me Chamerot's[27] address, I need to see him myself, Charpentier is a slowcoach.

I'll see you soon. *Tibissimi.*

G. Flaubert

I'm hacking away at *Bouvard and Pécuchet* again.

[Paris]
Saturday morning [21 April 1877]

My good old fellow,

I've just written to Pouchet asking him to be at my place tomorrow afternoon at about 4 o'clock, telling him that you need his advice. So try to be there.

Saint-Saens has forgotten me.[28] But knowing what the frenzy of first nights is like, I easily forgive him. I'd have been pleased to clap him, all the same!

N.B. Would there be any way of getting in to Massenet's rehearsal?[29]

Until tomorrow, and *ex imo*

G. Flaubert

Remind me to consult you over two passages of *A Simple Soul.*

[Paris]
Monday evening 9 o'clock [7 May 1877]

Alphonse Daudet: 18 rue des Vosges.

Why don't you come to the Charpentiers on Friday evening? (We shall just about all be there.) It's their last Friday.

Be ready to dine very shortly with Renan and me at Mme de

Tourbey's.[30] We must set up again this little 'family gathering' that didn't come off, as you weren't there.

Until tomorrow, at about 10 o'clock, at Victor Hugo's.

Your old G. Flaubert embraces you.

[Paris]
Thursday evening, midnight [10 May 1877]

My great good man,

I have just finished *Virgin Soil*. There's a book if ever there was one, and it purges one's brain from all previous reading! I'm dazed by it, although I have a perfect grasp of it as a whole. What a painter! And what a moralist you are, my dear, very dear friend! Too bad for your compatriots if they don't find your book wonderful. That's my opinion, and I know what I'm talking about.

Come on Saturday then, at about four o'clock, before you dine, so that we can talk about it quietly on our own. Would you prefer me to come to your place? I feel the need to embrace you.

I made a few pencil marks here and there. They only refer to trivial little points. The translation seemed adequate to me. I was so gripped by it though.

Bravo again. *Tibissimi*

G. Flaubert

I'm starting the second reading tomorrow morning. Oh the two little old men, and all the rest!

50 rue de Douai [Paris]
Saturday 19 May [1877]

My dear old fellow,

You must have said to yourself yesterday 'There's a joker for you! He doesn't come to the 'Feuille de rose' because he's got gout – and the following day he's going about the town!' Well, in fact I'm not such a joker as all that. I was not at all well yesterday when I went out (I was only away an hour, exactly, and you came 5 minutes too soon). As for the day before yesterday, Thursday, I was so wretched – my two feet were so painful – I felt so impotent, old, gouty, crippled – that the idea of going to see what was to be shown to us filled me with a dark melancholy: I don't doubt that I would have been bored, or worse, even if I had been able, with the two scourges I have in place of legs, to get up to the attic! I have decided to stay at home, like an old toad in his old damp hole. I shall make every effort to drag myself as far as your place tomorrow. Otherwise – farewell!

As soon as I can get into a railway carriage I shall set off, probably towards the end of next week.

However I should like to see you beforehand.

I embrace you – sadly.

Iv. Turgenev

50 rue de Douai [Paris]
Sunday morning [20 May 1877]

My dear friend,

Last night my foot swelled up again – and here I am confined to my armchair again. I'm not sure that I shall be able to leave the day after tomorrow; but in any case, I can't go out today.

I'm sending your manuscripts back to you. If you see Zola, tell him I'll send him some subjects for serials as soon as I've seen and talked to Stasyulevich. In the meantime – I've had an idea. What if he did a physiological study, using his inside knowledge, of Parisian journalism? It wouldn't be a news item, but it could be very curious. The Russian public loves that sort of thing.

Come then – farewell and until better times.

I embrace you.

Iv. Turgenev

P.S.   A thousand friendly greetings to Mme Commanville and her husband.

Les Frenes 16 rue de Mesmes Bougival
Wednesday 11 July 77

My dear old fellow,

I have been back here since yesterday! My journey was cut short by a violent attack of *gout* (!!!) at St Petersburg. I have brought you back a dressing-gown as fine as that worn by the Shah of Persia or rather the Khan of Bokhara! But I'm not sure whether you're at Croisset at the moment; drop me a line. We'll see if we can arrange a visit. For the moment my foot is still swollen and I walk with difficulty. Are you working? How is your health? My greetings to everyone – and I embrace you.

Iv. Turgenev

Croisset
Thursday 12 (July 1877]

My good dear old fellow,

Mme Viardot was so kind last Sunday as to tell me that she was expecting you the next day, that is Monday. As she added that you were ill, and not having heard from your Excellency, I am worried.

Anyway, are you back? How are you? That's what I'm ·dying to know. If you can hold a pen, then write to me straightaway. Thus we can write each other longer letters. I'm anxious about you, and I embrace you as I love you, that is with all my strength.

Your old

G. Flaubert

4 o'clock

I've just got your letter, and I've re-opened mine, my good dear old Turgenev, to tell you that I'm very relieved to know you're back. Look after your foot, then write me a long letter.

Bouvard and Pécuchet are coming on slowly, but they are coming on. At the end of next week I shall have finished the medicine section.

I shall be at Croisset until the middle of August. Everyone here is well.

Croisset
Thursday [19 July 1877]

It was very kind of you to write to me as soon as you got back, my good dear old fellow; but now I would like a few more details as to your large and exquisite person. And first of all, how is the foot? Has the swelling gone down? Is the attack over at last?

Did you get done in Russia what you wanted to do? Are you happy with the arrangements concerning your fortune? And holy literature, what's she up to in all this?

I await to see the famous *dressing-gown* before weeping with gratitude. But even now I thank you effusively: nothing could give me more pleasure, and *I'm dying* to try it on.

My medicine is finished (I'm talking about *B. and P.*). For the moment I'm working on the geology and archaeology (of Falaise and district). When this is finished, I shall make quite a long trip into Lower Normandy, then I shall come back here, to write the ending of this terrible Chapter II, which will have just about finished me off. And when it's finished (towards the New Year?) I shall be about a quarter of the way! One has to be mad to embark on such a work! Moreover this one may well be idiotic? In any case, it will be out of the ordinary.

What's more, I'm reading nothing outside of my immediate studies – what about you?

I should like to be at the elections to see the faces of the Macmahonites. Moral Order in the provinces goes so far as to ban charity meetings that aren't of a clerical nature. Oh Human Stupidity!

Farewell, my good dear old chap.

I embrace you.

Your

G. Flaubert

Les Frenes 16 rue de Mesmes Bougival

Thursday 24 July [1877]

My dear old fellow,

I didn't answer you straightaway as I was vaguely hoping to go to Croisset to bring you your dressing-gown myself; but this hope has faded away – for the moment – so I am writing to you and sending the dressing-gown by the railway. My foot is better – but it would still be impossible for me to walk much – I think I shall end up trying the new remedy that is much vaunted in the newspapers – its name begins with *sal* and ends in *ate*.[31] This blackguard gout is becoming semi-chronic and semi-accute in me, which is annoying. It's a pity B. and P. have *finished* their medical studies. I would have consulted them.

In Russia I got done a quarter of what I wanted to do – which is something. Naturally I didn't do the essential: I didn't see my brother. That's only normal.

I wish this war[32] would end, so that the exchange rate against the ruble would go back up. The present situation is completely paralysing my finances.

You are working – that's good; and your business affairs – the matter – you remember – that seemed so promising – how is it going?

My literature is for the moment in the depths of the deepest abyss.

I read Zola's little short story in 'L'Echo universel'.[33] The beginning especially is remarkable. My greetings to all.

I embrace you.

I.T.

P.S.   Let me know when you get the dressing-gown.

Croisset
Friday 4 o'clock [27 July 1877]

Splendid!

I'm overwhelmed by it. Thank you, my good dear old fellow. That really is a present! I would have answered you sooner if the railway brought parcels as far as here. But they don't, which means a delay of twenty-four if not thirty-six hours. (The station-master only wrote to me last night.)

This royal garment plunges me into dreams of absolutism and luxury. I should like to be naked underneath and harbour Circassian women inside it. Although the weather is stormy at the moment and I'm too hot, I'm wearing the said covering, and am thinking of how useful it will be to me this winter. Frankly you couldn't have given me a finer present.

I'm working on *B. and P.*'s geology; and on Monday I start writing again. When I've finished that chapter I shall give a great sigh of relief!

It's possible that I shall come and see you at Bougival towards the end of August. I'm not inviting you to Croisset at the moment, as your room is going to be taken by a friend of Caroline's. She'll stay for two weeks.

In September I shall make the archaeological and geological excursions in Lower Normandy, still all for my two fools. I'm afraid of being one myself. What a book! What an abyss (a wasps' nest or a latrine) I have stuffed myself into! There's no going back now.

But this autumn, the devil take it, you must come here and *stay*! An apparition of twenty-four or thirty-six hours is a cruel thing that upsets me in advance.

As for business affairs, they are dragging. The worst is over however. But the last 200 thousand francs are hard to find.

I'm reading *The Nabob* in *Le Temps*.[34] What do you think of it? I find the style rather slovenly, a bit childish.

The war in the East which doesn't concern me in the least annoys me. I wish the children of the Prophet a hearty thrashing, and let it be quick, so that we can have peace.

Were you, like me, outraged by Mme Gras?[35] She is the greatest criminal I know of.

No news from our friends, except for young Guy. He wrote to me recently. . . . That's all very well but. . . .[36] We are no longer at that stage, my good fellow!

Friendly greetings to all; and for you, a thousand tendernesses from your old

G. Flaubert

P.S. Indeed I succumb under the weight of your magnificence. I'm going to take the dressing-gown off. What is its local name and its homeland? Bokhara isn't it?

> Grand Hotel de la Place Royale Caen
> Friday evening 17 August 77

'Caen? Why Caen?' will you say, my dear old fellow? Why the devil is he in Caen? Ah, you see! The ladies of the Viardot family are to spend a fortnight at the seaside, either at Luc or at St-Aubin – and I have been sent on ahead to find something. I have brought your letter with me, and I hasten to say that I really *look forward* to having a visit from you, for I shall be back in Bougival by *Tuesday* – and I'll expect a note from you at Les Frenesas to when I should go and meet you in Paris in the Faubourg St Honoré. We shall have a lot to talk about – enough to make the walls of the room tremble!! So, from Tuesday onwards, I expect a note from you.
I embrace you.

> Your
> I. Turgenev

> Les Frenes Bougival
> Thursday, 30 August 1877

My dear friend,
When you talk to me, you think you're having dealings with a human being: think again – I'm nothing but an old gouty vessel. That is to say it's come on again violently, the very evening of the day we had lunch together – and that I've been laid up since then. This last night it moved up from the heel to the knee – and it has probably not yet finished its travels. So if you want to see me, you'll have to do as Muhammad and go to the mountain.
Thereupon I embrace you and wish you many good things – but not the gout.

> Your
> I. Turgenev

> Les Frenes Bougival
> Saturday 8 a.m. 1 September [1877]

My dear old fellow,
I'm writing this to stop you 'going to the mountain' if you were

thinking of doing so. I've decided to drag myself into Paris, on my crutches, to have a consultation with Dr Sée; otherwise I would have had to put it off until Wednesday, as he spends Sundays and Mondays at Trouville and doesn't see patients on Tuesdays. I don't know what time he'll let me go, and it's impossible for me to climb up to your 5th floor – so our meeting, dinner etc. will all come to nothing. After the age of 40 there is only one word to sum up the basis of life: *Renunciation.*

I embrace you and wish you good health, activity etc. etc.

Your old

I. Turgenev

[Paris]
Thursday [6 September 1877]

Well, my poor old fellow, how are you? What did your doctor say? It upsets me terribly to know that you're always suffering.

In a week's time, I shan't be far off going back to Croisset, and from there to set off for Lower Normandy.

I've seen young de Maupassant, back from Switzerland which he has sullied with sundry horrors.

The death of father Thiers[37] worries me. I'm afraid it may serve the interests of the infamous Party of Law and Order.

There's going to be a new edition of the *Three Tales* and *Saint Anthony.*

I embrace you.

Your

G. Flaubert

Send me a note to 240 Faubourg Saint-Honoré.

[Paris]
Wednesday 12 [September 1877]

My old darling,

I turned up at the rue de Douai to see you yesterday. I learnt that you had been there the day before and that the gout is leaving you alone now.

If you should return to Paris on Friday or Saturday, drop me a line to let me know; I'll come and see you in the afternoon, and don't be surprised at my long stay in the capital: I am delayed here (*inter nos*) *Veneris causa*!!![38]

I'm finally leaving on Sunday; and on Tuesday or Wednesday at the latest your friend begins *B. and P.*'s archaeological and geological excursions.

This winter you must keep your old promise: come to Croisset *for a long time*, settle down and hammer away alongside me.

All the best.

Your
G. Flaubert

[Croisset]
[17 September 1877]

Just a note, dear friend, to tell you that I called on you on Saturday, the day before yesterday.

The day after tomorrow I start the excursions for *B. and P.* which will last a good fortnight. I hope to have a letter from you on my return.

What do you think of Daudet's new novel?[39] Read, *I beg you The Loves of Philip* by Octave Feuillet.[40] What a nullity!

When is the marriage of Mlle Viardot, and when shall we see each other? You know I don't want you at Croisset if it's for twenty-four or forty-eight hours. Such a ridiculously short stay *takes all the pleasure away* for me.

I embrace you.

Your old fellow who loves you dearly

G. Flaubert

Tell me about Russia. There'll be no end to this dreadful war then!

[Croisset]
Friday [5 October 1877]

Why have I not heard from you, my good dear old fellow? I expected to find a letter from you on my return. Could it be that you are ill?

I have been dragging myself about for two weeks: now I'm going to have to work like a madman. What are you up to? etc., etc.

My nephew's *affairs* seem to be on the *right* track. But what about politics? My hatred for the Moral Order and our 'Bayard'[41] is choking me and wearing me down.

I embrace you.

Your old
G. Flaubert

The Chalet Les Frenes Bougival
Friday 5 October [1877]

My dear friend,
Just a note to tell you not to be surprised at my silence. For several reasons which I'll tell you about when we see each other – I've been in the doldrums all this time and unfit for human company.

As soon as possible, I'll come and see you. I'll give you advance warning.

I'm reading nothing, I'm doing nothing – and on top of all that I'm perfectly well, thanks to the salicylate.

Mlle Viardot's wedding has been put off for a while.

Work hard – for both of us. I embrace you.

Your faithful
I.T.

Croisset
Tuesday [9 October 1877]

What's the matter then my old darling? Who is upsetting you and what's holding you up? The tone of your note of Friday worries me.

I'm thinking about you a lot and I'd like to keep you all to myself for *several* days.

In spite of the brutalising effect of politics, I have the feeling that I'm going to be able to work.

I embrace you in spite of my cold caught a week ago on a visit to a druid encampment.

All the best.

Your
G. Flaubert

50 rue de Douai Paris
Thursday 8 November 77

My good old fellow,
I really must write to you, if only to find out how much longer you're planning to stay at Croisset, because I *want* to come and see you, whatever happens!

We left the country ten days ago and are definitively installed here now.

My health is good, thanks to the sodium salicylate which I have been taking for two months and which seems to have eliminated the gout.

My principal source of distress has been the breaking off of the marriage of Mme Viardot's second daughter – with a boy who was my protégé and whom I liked. All this happened before my very eyes – there were some psychological anomalies that I would have preferred to meet with elsewhere.

We'll talk about all that and other things as well. I've seen and see nobody. Zola should be back; I expect I'll go and knock on his door one of these days.

I hope you are well and that you are working hard. Chamerot told me that you *Three Tales* are being reprinted, so much the better!

I embrace you. Your old

I. Turgenev

P.S. Politics is a fine mess, isn't it? I've always been convinced that this government would last – and that a blockhead, strategically placed is stronger than a whole nation.

[Croisset]
Saturday evening [17 November 1877]

What a strange fellow you are! For the last week I've been expecting a letter from you twice daily announcing your arrival. Are you ill? What's the matter?

I'd rather see you now than later, for I'm not writing at the moment. I'm reading and taking notes and going to the library in Rouen. After which I shall tackle the archaeology chapter. Come *illico* then, than is Tuesday or Wednesday. The Commanvilles are leaving here on Tuesday morning and are sorry not to see you.

On Thursday next I *must* go to Rouen for two hours to 'honour with my presence' the unveiling of the bust of old Pouchet at the Natural History Museum. If you're here, you can come with me.

I expect an immediate answer from you and I embrace you.

Your old

G. Flaubert

What a good gossip we'll have! Arrange things so as to stay for some time, damn it all! And don't upset me in advance with a premature departure.

[Croisset]
Wednesday evening [28 November 1877]

My poor fellow, it really upsets me to know that you are ill. If your hands aren't painful, and if you can manage to write to me, send me a long epistle to keep me company in my solitude.

I have just read *The Nabob*. It's moving and has quality, but here and there there are things I don't like. A pretty fine book, all in all.

Your friend is somewhat knocked up by an excess of labour. I'm starting to have trouble sleeping, as *B. and P.*'s archaeology is preoccupying me excessively.

Let me have news of you and try to be patient. I pity you and I embrace you.

Your old
G. Flaubert

50 rue de Douai Paris
Wednesday 5 December 77

My good old fellow,

I'm still in the same horizontal position! I have had a relapse since I wrote to you. I'm no longer in pain – but I'm starting to wonder how one uses one's legs; a man who walks on crutches seems like a colossus and a hero to me.

I imagine I am like this to keep poor old France company, for she neither can move a limb. What a situation to be in my dear friend! We've never seen the like. An engine that's heading at full steam into an abyss, while the driver quietly scratches his backside, or sits with arms folded. And this lie, this barefaced lie oozing out of everything, like water dripping from a frozen log on a fire. I repeat, we've never seen anything like it.[42]

Mme Commanville had the goodness and grace to visit the invalid. I found her radiant with health. I've seen Zola as well, who is definitely going to write a play for Sarah Bernhardt.

I've just finished *The Nabob*. It's a book that contains things *above* Daudet's usual level, but other things that are well *below*. His observations are superb; but the imaginative part is slight and insipid – and not even original. In spite of everything, the good aspects of the book are so good, that I think I'm going to make up my mind to write him a *truthful* letter, which will give him both pleasure and pain. Perhaps after all, I won't.

And you – are you working? Mme Commanville told me you are . . . so much the better. Take advantage of things while no infirmity has got hold of you. For once it has – there's an end to things. It fills you with resignation and humility, which is perhaps excellent from a Christian point of view, but not worth a damn to the man who still hopes to achieve something.

You'll come back for the New Year won't you?

Farewell, I embrace you. I am not sad but I feel no joy: I feel like a shade from the Elysian fields in Gluck's Orpheus. I must have their look of 'profound' amazement and 'profound' indifference, as Jules Simon,[43] now Macmahon's minister, used to say. Jules Simon a minister![43] Can you beat that?

All the best

Iv. Turgenev

Croisset
Saturday 8 [December 1877]

My niece had sent me a pitiful description of your dear and gigantic person, but your letter yesterday, without cheering me up, at least quietened my fears: at last, or at least for the moment, you're not in pain. Ah, my poor old fellow, how I pity you to be so constantly plagued with this damned gout! Can you work a bit, read, dream about literary matters?

I think exactly like you about *The Nabob*. It's uneven. It's not only a question of seeing, but what one has seen has to be arranged and blended. From my point of view Reality should be no more than a *springboard*. Our friends are convinced that that alone makes up the whole of Art. This materialism annoys me, and nearly every Monday, I get an attack of irritation when I read dear Zola's serials. After the Realists, we have the Naturalists and the Impressionists. What progress! A bunch of clowns who want to increase their own importance and make us all believe that they've invented the wheel.

As for me, my good fellow, I'm working hard, hammering away, slaving like Niggerdom personified. What will be the result? Ah, there's the hitch. At times I feel *crushed* by the mass of this work, which may well be a failure; if it is, there'll be no half measures. So far it's not going too badly. But later on? I've still got loads of things to read, and to vary loads of things that create a similar effect.

Anyway, in a fortnight I shall be about a third of the way through the book. Another three years of hard labour. For the moment I'm dabbling in celtic archaeology with B. and P., what a laugh.

And I am miraculously well, but I no longer sleep, not at all. And towards evening I get quite violent pains in the back of the head.

This morning I see in *Le Bien Public* that perhaps we have a government. Bayard is not letting go. I fear some underhand business or that the good citizens will end up regretting the passing of the Empire and want it back again. So, *de profundis*.

Here at Croisset, the rain never stops, we're under water. But as I don't go out, I don't care, and then I have your dressing-gown. I bless you twice daily for that gift: in the morning when I get out of bed, and towards 5 or 6 in the evening when I wrap myself up in it to 'have a nap' on my sofa.

I think I must abandon all hope of seeing you here at home between now and the New Year? My plan is to arrive in Paris at that very time.

Until then, dear good old fellow. I embrace you.

Your
G. Flaubert

[Paris]
Sunday evening 11 o'clock [13 January 1878]

My good fellow,

I am not cross with you. I'm writing a note in reply, and I continue to find you the most incomprehensible of fellows. Well, I choose *next Saturday*. If you let me down on that day, I shall ask for a consultation of the Princes of Science.

Get hold of this evening's copy of Zola's theatrical serial and see what he says about *Macbeth*.[44] He doesn't find Shakespeare lively because he's not contemporary! Read it as a punishment.

Your
G. Flaubert

50 rue de Douai Paris
Monday 14 January 78

My dear friend,

I am indeed a strange creature, but less so than you think this time.

I had told you that the great Khanikov[45] had invited me for today. I could have got out of it if he hadn't purposely asked other people . . . but imagine, two mathematicians expressly invited! My reputation (for punctuality) is already so bad, that I should have been damned for all time.

I read Zola's serial . . . What do you expect? I pity him. Yes it's compassion that he inspires in me: and I fear that he's never read

Shakespeare. There is an element of original sin there, that he'll never rid himself of.

So, it's for SATURDAY!

It's I who will be on time that day.

Your

Iv. Turgenev

[Paris]
Saturday night [26 January 1878]

My good fellow,

You can't be ill, since you called on me today, and I suspect that tomorrow you want to give yourself up to *some depravity*, that is to listen to some music or see some paintings, *inferior arts*.

As for *Bouvard and Pécuchet*, I'll read you what's finished whenever you like. Come and dine here, and we'll divide the reading into two sessions. I only have Tuesday, Thursday and Saturday free this week. Do you want to put it off until next week?

I wanted to go and see Mme Viardot today. Give her my apologies, but I was detained by Renan who read something to me.

My niece is sorry to have missed your visit. Her day is *Wednesday*.

I shall try to come and see you on Tuesday afternoon, towards four or five o'clock.

At the moment I am lost in i) historical criticism, ii) celticism, iii) the story of the Duke of Angoulême!!! That book's heavy. Shall I have the strength to carry on with it? I must be mad to have embarked on it. However?

Farewell, my dear good old fellow. It's not kind not to come tomorrow. I embrace you.

Your

G. Flaubert

[Paris]
[Sunday 14 April 1878]

No, my good fellow! Don't come tomorrow because every day this week, except Friday, I'm spending my afternoons at the Theatrical Library reading stupid historical plays.

But try to come on *Friday* at about 2 o'clock. If one of these evenings (except Wednesday) you are free, come. In any case I expect you on Friday at about 2 o'clock.

All the best my dear friend.

Your

G. Flaubert

[Paris]
Friday 5 o'clock 19 April 1878

My old darling,

The sale of your pictures, which upsets me because it's painful for you, doubtless made you forget that today, Friday, you were supposed to come to my place at 3 o'clock to receive from your friend literary confidences concerning *B. and P.*

For my part, I forgot to warn you that: *Thursday next*, very probably, you will be invited to dine at Mme Brainne's with Guy, G. Pouchet, Mme Pasca and me.[46] I shall know about it definitely tomorrow, and I'll tell you on Sunday. (I should have let you know *ten* days ago.)

Arrange things so that you can spare me two hours next Monday afternoon.

I embrace you. Until Sunday.

Your

G. Flaubert

[Paris]
[April 1878]

I waited until the last minute, but I must take the decision. You won't see me this evening. My coughing would prevent you from eating. A pulse of a hundred, lost voice, in short, a raging attack of 'flu.

All my apologies to our friends.

G. Flaubert

I feel so awful I'm having a job to write this letter.

[Paris]
[May 1878]

I don't know if the dinner will come off. Daudet has the 'flu and wrote that he wouldn't come. I await Zola and Goncourt to know their decision. I'll let you have it this evening.

Yours

G. Flaubert

I expect you tommorrow at 1 o'clock.

[Paris]
[1878]

Your telegramme of yesterday is not clear. 'Come tomorrow.' Where to? To Bougival? That's not possible. If it's Paris, fine. So tomorrow, on the off chance, I'll ring at your door in the rue de Douai, at about three o'clock in the afternoon. But don't change your plans on my account, because I won't be able to spare you much time.

All the best my dear fellow.

G. Flaubert

[Paris]
Sunday [September 1878]

I was unpleasantly surprised not to find you in Paris the day before yesterday, my good dear old fellow. What an abominable thing this gout is!

When shall we see each other now? Doubtless at Croisset? For I shall barely stop here on my way back from Saint-Gratien.

I embrace you tenderly.

Your

G. Flaubert

One of these days I might call at the rue de Douai on the off chance . . . Poor friend! How I pity you.

[Paris]
[1878]

Mme Mazeline[47] lives at 134 boulevard Haussmann. Her day is Friday.

Yesterday while you were coming here, I was on my way to your place, which proves we felt an equal desire to see each other, my dear old fellow.

I'm sending the bottom part of your sketch to Daudet.
Until tomorrow and all the best

G. Flaubert

[Paris]
[1878]

You reduce me to *tears* my good Turgenev. It's not possible to be nicer. What a friend I have in you! I embrace you.
I'll see you tomorrow won't I?

G. Flaubert

IV
June 1878–May 1880

On the literary front, this last period of the correspondence between Flaubert and Turgenev is dominated by the figures of Bouvard and Pécuchet, the eponymous heroes of Flaubert's last and unfinished work. He felt exhausted by the scale of the work he had undertaken, and, one feels, risked becoming a bore to his friends by the extent to which he lamented over the slowness of the book's progress.

Turgenev, for his part, wrote little at this time; this formerly prolific writer of fiction now concentrated his efforts on short prose poems that are, for the most part, a powerful distillation of unrelieved pessimism. This emerges through the themes of death, old age and the vanity of human affairs in general. Turgenev had planned to call this collection *Senilia*, but his publisher advised against it.

On Saturday, 25 January 1879, Flaubert slipped on a patch of ice in his garden at Croisset and fell, breaking a leg. The news of this accident appeared in *Le Figaro* of the 28th. Turgenev, made anxious by the news, arrived at Croisset on Monday, 3 February, for a two-day stay. Besides consoling his friend, the principal purpose of the visit was to try and persuade Flaubert (whose finances were still in a far from healthy state) to accept a post of librarian at the Bibliothèque Mazarine in Paris. It was generally acknowledged that the incumbent was on his death bed. Turgenev saw this as a sinecure, offering the advantages of a regular income, and a prestigious apartment overlooking the Seine. He imagined that the most difficult part of the operation would be to persuade the proud Flaubert to accept the state's munificence; he even wildly exaggerated the amount of the stipend to strengthen his case. Along with Zola and Flaubert's publisher Charpentier, Turgenev took a great deal of trouble over this affair; he wrote letters every day to Zola and Flaubert, put off his journey to Russia and paid many calls. Yet his efforts were to be all in vain. What Turgenev had not conceived of, was that the Third Republic would not gladly and enthusiastically honour its great novelist, should the novelist but wish it. He had obtained Flaubert's consent with surprising ease (he was, as he commented to Caroline, won over by his Russian friend's 'eloquence and tenderness') but Gambetta, who now dominated the political scene, had other plans. The post went ultimately to the son-in-law of one of his ministers, in recompense for political favours received.

Turgenev was to make two more visits to Croisset that year: two days at the beginning of May (the occasion for a thank-you gift of a Swedish fish delicacy) and again in December to celebrate Flaubert's fifty-eighth birthday on the 12th, and once more gastronomic parcels followed. This was to be the last meeting between the two friends. In fact, the last letter written to Flaubert by Turgenev was never read by him, for he died at home at Croisset on 8 May 1880, two days after Turgenev had written to him from the depths of Russia. He was to learn the sad news at Spasskoye from the columns of the newspaper *The Voice*.

Croisset
Thursday 20 June [1878]

My good old fellow,

I thought you were in Germany, and I was expecting a letter from you one of these days giving me details of your devilish gout, when the reverberations of the Press, penetrating as far as my solitude, brought me the news of your oratorical triumphs.[1] Bravo, my old darling! Your little speech is charming. I have only one regret, not to have been there to applaud you.

As for me, nothing new. *B. and P.* are coming on quite well. I hope to have finished my chapter towards the end of July. I shall then be *half* way through my book. Your friend is patient, and my poor eyes are starting to wear out.

My niece and her husband are coming back here on Monday, but will soon leave me, I think, to go and take the waters, one to the Vosges, the other to the Pyrenees. As for me, I shan't budge.

Where will this note find you? May it bring with it all my tenderness! I embrace you.

G. Flaubert

No news from our Sunday friends. I only know that Mme Daudet has re-given birth.

I think it's odd that Taine has been beaten by Henri Martin.[2]

Les Frenes 16 rue de Mesmes Bougival
Sunday 23 June [1878]

I also, my dear friend, thought I would be in Germany at the present time: not a bit of it! I let myself get involved with this business of the International Congress which *won't and can't produce any result* – and here I am making speeches and so on and so forth! Oh my friend, what a curious thing a deliberative assembly is! There is Victor Hugo, who yesterday made a superb speech; the speech is acclaimed, we vote on its printing as in the Constituent Assembly! And five minutes later, we vote on a resolution diametrically opposed to his speech – and he votes for it himself!! We have a commission that sits every day (I am its vice-president) – we mark time like idiots, and I begin to believe that to all intents and purposes we are. I've had enough to it, and I'm leaving for Carlsbad on *Thursday*, where I beg you to write to me (C., Bohemia, poste restante). The water I shall drink there is perhaps also an illusion – but it's not so obvious.

As for you, I wish you good health and patience, with all my heart.

I saw Zola for a minute; he has bought a little house near Maisons-Lafitte, and is going to move in there.

H. Martin is certainly not a greater writer – but you must admit that to see Taine taking Thiers' place is monstrous! Personally I like Martin a lot and am pleased at his success.

I embrace you.

Iv. Turgenev

Croisset
Tuesday evening 10 July [1878]

Well, my good dear old fellow, how are you? Has the gout gone, or is it at least leaving you in peace? And how is your mood?

As for me there is nothing new. I'm still working doggedly at my awful book – at the end of this month, I hope to have finished Chapter V! After that one I shall have V more, without counting the volume of notes. On certain days I feel crushed by this burden. It seems to me that I have no more marrow in my bones, and I carry on like an old post horse, worn out but courageous. What a task my good fellow! Provided that it's not pure madness? It's the very conception of the book that worries me. Anyway! May God's grace prevail! There's no time to think about that now. Never mind, I often wonder whether I wouldn't have done better to spend so much time on something else.

My niece is here at Croisset; and since she's started drinking cider again (you may be disdainful) no longer suffers from stomach pains. She is having the billiard room arranged as a studio and is going to take up painting again. She and her husband, knowing that I am writing to you, beg me to send their greetings to my great friend.

I've received a terribly sad letter from my disciple Guy de

Maupassant. His mother's health is giving him cause for concern, and he himself feels ill. His Ministry (the Navy) is getting on his nerves and is overtaxing him so that he can no longer work, and 'those ladies' are incapable of cheering him up! Moreover, as 'the whole of Europe envies us them' even more than our institutions, they are so over-worked at the moment, that you can't get anywhere near them. After the Exhibition, there will be a good twenty thousand of them dead from overwork (*sic*).

Zola is the owner of a country house, whose floors, being rotten, nearly collapsed under him. 'Le Bien Public' is just about dead as you know, but he (Zola) is going to flourish the banner of naturalism in the *Voltaire*, a new publication.

Mme Alphonse Daudet has been delivered of a boy. That's all I know of my friends.

Dead calm on the political horizon it seems? Yesterday there were elections for the Chamber, where the Friends of Law and Order were undone.

I don't know if Catulle's *Capitaine Fracasse* has been a success.[3]

The summer is dreadful. Rain every day! I wanted to play at being Triton in the Seine, but the temperature is against it.

When are you coming back? As for me, I shall not budge from my old homestead between now and the end of the year, except perhaps for a fortnight in September to go to the princess's and to visit the Exhibition.

Will you come and see me this autumn? You know very well I shan't invite you, as you are too disagreeable with your preoccupations about leaving. If you can only stay for less than a week, I don't want you! It would none the less be a great delight to me to have you, my good dear old fellow. In the winter we see each other in unfavourable circumstances, that is, with too many people around us. Our friends are very nice . . . , but after all none of them is *you*.

Keep happy. Write to me, and think of your

G. Flaubert who loves you and embraces you.

[Croisset]
Wednesday morning 9 o'clock [17 July 1878]

Your letter dated the 15th arrived only today the 17th; and will this one reach you in time to greet you before your departure?

There has been one from me waiting for you at Carlsbad for two weeks. *Demand it.* It was quite long I remember. Man of devious plans, I embrace you. Write to me as soon as you are in Russia.

I finished my fifth chapter yesterday, the one about literature. I am well, but worked to death. This book is heavy going.

All the best, my good old fellow. Have a good journey and come back quickly.

> Your
> G. Flaubert

Mme Régnier[4]

> 50 rue de Douai Paris
> Saturday 9 November 78

My dear old fellow,

Is it you Rhadamite, after so many misfortunes? After such a long silence, after trips to Russia and to England, to the back of beyond – yes, it's me; and I've come to say that I've only been settled in Paris since yesterday, that I want to hear from you, you must tell me how much longer you're staying at Croisset – for I suppose that's where you are, and that I want to come and see you. My health is quite good – and I can walk on my own like a three-year-old. I'll add no more today, as I feel somewhat dazed – and I await your answer.

I embrace you.

> Your
> Iv. Turgenev

> [Croisset]
> Sunday [10 November 1878]

Ah! At last! I was going to write to Mme Viardot again. I had asked Maupassant to call at your house. I was imagining all sorts of possibilities. In short I uttered a cry of joy when I saw your handwriting this morning.

I have wandered less than you; for except for three weeks in September spent partly in Paris and partly at Saint-Gratien, and three days recently at Etretat, I have been at my desk for the last six months. My fellows are giving me devilish trouble. At times I can't bear it any longer and I've still two years to go. What a book! And how mad I must be to have embarked on it!

Moreover my life is not much fun. *Business matters* are not sorting themselves out – the very opposite. Resignation has come; but at times it lets me down, and then I reflect bitterly on the past and think about death. Then I get back to work again.

I don't count on being back in Paris before the beginning or even the end of February. I want to have finished my chapter on *Love*!!! The one on Politics will be finished in a fortnight.

You well know that I don't count at all on a visit from you, in spite of your promises. And what's more, you're like Galatea: we hardly catch sight of you and then you've gone! However . . . ?

If you are not too busy (but you are a busy man) write me a long epistle. It is not kind to have left your old fellow without news for such a long time; he embraces you and cherishes you.

G. Flaubert

50 rue de Douai Paris
Wednesday 27 November 78

My dear old fellow,

In response to your little note, whose sadness upset me, I wanted to drop in on you unannounced at Croisset – and if I didn't do so – it was for good reason. I had to bury an old friend of forty years (forty years of friendship) Khanikov, who let himself die at Rambouillet, in the most miserable house I've ever seen. The weather was bad at Père-Lachaise[5] – mud underfoot, and a sort of hail or snow falling, an awful dirty fog enveloping everything. They had a terrible job to get the enormous and heavy coffin down into the gaping hole. I said a few words of farewell on the edge of the grave, on a heap of muddy, slippery sods. I spoke bareheaded and caught quite a bad cold which is confining me to my room and preventing me from coming to Croisset. However, I'm getting better, and *certainly* next week will not go by without your having seen me in your *house at Croisset*. I can see from here the sceptical smile on your lips; and I must admit that you have a right to that smile, given the number of times I have not kept my word; and yet – you'll see! You'll see!

Zola is not yet back in Paris; I haven't seen Daudet, Goncourt came here yesterday to get a bit of local colour – southern Russia, names of gypsies etc. I found him in good health – a bit thinner – and still the same shining dull eyes – not nice at all. He spoke about you in a very understanding way.

I have just turned 60, my dear old fellow . . . This is the start of the tail-end of life. A Spanish proverb says that the tail is the hardest part to flay. At the same time it's the part that gives least pleasure and satisfaction. Life becomes completely self-centred – a defensive struggle with death; and this exaggeration of the personality means that it ceases to be of interest, even to the person in question. But you are already not very cheerful – without me adding this lugubrious note; pretend I said nothing.

When we see each other I shall have a *lot* of things to tell you about my two journeys to Russia and to England; so make me talk.

Everyone here is well and sends you their greetings. And I embrace you. *I'll see you soon.* I'll let you know the day before.

Your

Iv. Turgenev

Croisset

Sunday night 1 December [1878]

My good dear old fellow,

In my last letter, I begged you to come. Well *don't come this week.* My head would not be clear, and you would not be well received. I – or rather we – are submerged with worries; but I hope it's the end. Ah, my poor friend, what a burden life is!

I ask you and even *beg* you to save your kind visit for the very near future, in a week or ten days perhaps? I'll let you know as soon as I have calmed down.

I really need to have a long chat with you.

I embrace you.

Your

G. Flaubert

50 rue de Douai Paris

Wednesday 4 December 78

Certainly, my dear friend, I'll wait until you tell me to come and I hope you will do so soon. I am very disturbed to learn that you are in such an awful state – and what's more I hope that you are exaggerating it a bit, as a result of your nerves. As for the *heaviness* of life – nothing is light once you're past fifty. So I'll see you soon – won't I?

I embrace you.

Your old

Iv. Turgenev

Croisset

Sunday 22 December [1878]

My dear old fellow,

My silence must surprise you? My excuse, alas, is a valid one. I have had such *money worries*, such violent anxieties, that I'm amazed that I haven't gone completely off my head. The hope of recovering my fortune is completely vanished, and my fate won't finally be decided until the end of January. I'll tell you all about it when we're sitting at the fireside. Don't say anything to the Others.

I've never felt the need for anyone as much as I feel the need for you. The company of my dear Turgenev will do my heart, mind and nerves good. I expect you at the beginning of January, not before, (i) because it's going to be the New Year, (ii) you would be too uncomfortable here in this awful weather, (iii) my niece and her husband are going to start preparing to leave for Paris. I shall not be there until the beginning of February.

So, I expect you in two or three weeks. I shall have three chapters of *B. and P.* to read to you. I have three more left. But before starting to write again, I need a good three or four months of reading.

No news from our friends.

Ah, my poor old fellow, Providence (or what we call Providence) has given me some fine insults to pocket. I have been beset with both crushing blows and petty annoyances, even Charpentier (his son!) prefers Sarah Bernardt's [*sic*] literature to mine![6]

All this has left me with a jaundiced view of things; but like Thomas Diafoirus I have 'girded myself up to face the difficulties'[7] and I have continued to scribble on paper, imagining that it was important.

I shall see you soon, shan't I? I embrace and hug you.

Your old

G. Flaubert

My respects to Mme Viardot.

50 rue de Douai Paris
Tuesday 7 January 1879

Well, my friend, still no letter? What's more it's probably for the best, for if you had written to me two weeks or ten days ago, I shouldn't have been able to come, as I have been in bed with the gout. The attack was very violent – but short – and for the last five days I've been able to put my boots on and walk like a normal human being. Let me have news of you in any case – and don't forget that you promised to come to Paris at the beginning of February. Our poor dinners are in jeopardy.

I've only seen Goncourt once; I've had a note from Daudet who is suffering badly with rheumatism in his *right* arm; as for Zola – he has been back in Paris for 4 days – and I have just seen him. He is very portly – he has just finished having a country house built – and in ten days 'L'Assommoir' is being performed! He has promised me a seat in the stalls for the first night. There'll probably be a real uproar; what's more, he knows it and doesn't care. He doesn't care either about the fuss his Russian articles have caused, and the violent attacks by Ulbach and Claretie etc. But I realise that you hardly get any papers at home, and are perhaps ignorant of the whole affair.[8] We'll talk about it when we see each other, if it hasn't all died down by then.

It upsets me to see you in such a sticky situation from which you cannot extricate yourself! But you mustn't fret over it – in spite of everything – and I'm pleased to know that you're getting on with your work.

Nevertheless there are things that I don't understand. What is it to you if Charpentier publishes Sarah Bernhardt – and what kind of petty annoyance is that? This book, as stupidly written as it is wretchedly illustrated by M. Clairin, is already more forgotten than last year's fashions.

And what do you have to say about the vote the day before yesterday?

Mme Viardot sends you her regards and I embrace you.

Your

Iv. Turgenev

Croisset

Thursday [9 January 1879]

My good dear old fellow,

I wrote to you shortly before the New Year. You didn't get my letter then!

In that letter I told you I was counting on seeing you *here* at the beginning of January? Can you come now? Would it inconvenience you? It would be a *charitable act* to pay me a visit, for I really want or rather need to see you.

It's not possible for me to be in Paris before the end of February at the earliest, on account of my dreadful *business affairs*. I foresee big problems. So! And if the typhoid fever currently raging in Rouen were to carry me off, it would be good riddance as far as I'm concerned. But no! It's not spreading beyond the city boundary, remaining confined to the homeland of Pierre Corneille and Pouyer-Quertier.

You ask me what is it to me if Charpentier publishes Sarah Bernhardt? Let me tell you that the said Charpentier had solemnly promised me last September (for the third time) and sworn to bring out an edition of *Saint Julian the Hospitaler* embellished with a chromolithograph, a de luxe edition. As it's very expensive, he was reluctant and preferred to publish Sarah's rubbish. I was counting on getting a bit of money from that quarter – and nothing. It's like Dalloz at the *Moniteur* who didn't even deign to read the manuscript I sent him, a further blow to my financial situation. In short I'm not having much joy.

Nevertheless, I'm working like an ox. I have three chapters to read to you, Literature, Politics and Love! Now I'm working on the last three: Philosophy, Religion, Morality.

Your friend is lost in metaphysics, and at present I'm reading amongst other things, Viardot's little book[9] which seems to me even better than the first time. Compliment him on it again for me.

I don't understand how Zola's article caused so much scandal, for all in all his criticisms were quite mild! But people are so cowardly and so hypocritical that frankness seems out of place. We are supposed to admire mediocrity.

Monday's vote pleased me, as a blow to the party of law and order. But I am afraid of a backlash. It's the Republic that is going to become the party of law and order! Provided it doesn't become that of Stupidity!

Present my respects to Mme Viardot. I embrace you tenderly.

Your
G. Flaubert

I am all alone here; my niece has been in Paris since New Year's Day.

Come. I'll try to arrange things so you won't be cold, and you'll write back straightaway, won't you.

50 rue de Douai Paris
Saturday 11 January 79

My dear friend,

I shall come and see you as soon as this cold and snowy weather is over – probably towards the end of next week. Naturally you'll get advance warning. I also have the greatest desire to see you and to talk to you.

I didn't know that Mme Commanville was back in Paris; I shall go and call on her tomorrow.

You are in a sorry state my poor dear old fellow but you have your health, your work – and true friends: and that makes life possible.

Above all, don't eat yourself up with anxiety; it's the only thing that man succumbs to.

The whole Viardot family sends you friendly greetings.

As for me, I embrace you.

Your

Iv. Turgenev

50 rue de Douai Paris

Tuesday 21 January 79

My good old fellow,

You are perhaps wondering why there are no signs of life from me? Alas, my friend, decidedly I am nothing more than an invalid who can no longer 'undertake' to do anything. It's nearly two weeks since the gout seized hold of me again – and it's only since yesterday that I've been able to walk in my bedroom – with the help of crutches of course. I wasn't able to go to the first night of L'Assommoir which, duly expurgated it would seem, had all the success of a good old melodrama. Yesterday I received news of the death of my brother; that causes me much grief – retrospective and personal. We saw each other only rarely – and we had hardly anything in common . . . but a brother – it's sometimes less, but it's something other than a friend. Less strong and more intimate. My brother died rich with a fortune of millions – but he leaves it all to relations of his wife. He left me (according to what he wrote to me) 250,000 francs in his will – (it's about a twentieth of his fortune) – but as the people he mixed with in the last years of his life are rogues, I shall probably have to be on the spot without delay – my brother's legacy could well disappear into thin air. So, in ten days' time, I shall perhaps be on the road to Moscow. In that case, when shall we see each other again? For there can be no thought of going to Croisset now. And yet I have the greatest desire to see you. Do you really need to stay there until the end of February? What a sad winter! No mole leads a more secluded life than I do. Being alone, all alone – and doing nothing – that really gives one a taste – and an aftertaste – of one's uselessness. After all! Patience!

Happily all are well here.

Drop me a line. I hope that your work is coming on steadily.

I embrace you.

Your

I. Turgenev

50 rue de Douai Paris
Friday 24 January 79

My dear old fellow,
I received your letter, and yesterday Mme Commanville was kind enough to come and see me. We had a long chat. Naturally you were the principal subject of conversation. I found her in good health and ready to work. I shall return her visit as soon as I can walk without a stick, and more particularly, climb stairs.

It is not impossible that my journey to Russia will be delayed: everything depends on the letters I get from over there. In that case I shall certainly come to Croisset. Unfortunately the father of the heiress is a rogue, who wants nothing more than to rob me. Perhaps my presence will prevent him from doing so. I don't really believe it will – but perhaps it is necessary for me to pretend to believe it.

Your niece told me that you are in good health: that's the essential. You don't like walking, but you should force yourself to do it. I was once in prison – in solitary confinement – for more than a month: the room was small, the heat stifling. Twice a day I carried 104 cards (two packs) – one by one – from one end of the room to the other . . . that made 208 round trips; 416 a day, the round trip was 8 paces, that made 3,300, nearly 2 kilometres! Let this ingenious calculation give you courage! The day I didn't take my walk, all the blood went to my head!

I cut out for you from a newspaper the enclosed article which seems to be the work of a complete pompous ass! Add it to your collection.

I shall write to you soon, as soon as I know something for certain.
In the meantime I embrace you.

Your
Iv. Turgenev

[Croisset]
Thurdsay midday [30 January 1879]

No, my good old fellow, don't come. I'd be too, too sad to see you go; and frankly it isn't worth the trouble to come for a visit of two hours. When I can get up and have a long chat with you, which will be in about two weeks' time, I'll summon you, if you're going to Russia.

Did you know that I broke my leg five minutes after reading the letter in which you recommended walking to me?!! Funny isn't it?

It'll be six weeks or two months before I'm able to walk, and I shall limp for a long time. I am as well as can be expected, and I embrace you.

Your old cripple
G. Flaubert

Le Figaro being stupid enough to publish news of my accident, all my friends are worried, and I received fifteen letters yesterday and eleven this morning. There are the benefits of journalism for you. What right has Villemessant[10] to my leg? Note that he thinks he's doing me an honour and giving me pleasure. I found that paragraph *very distasteful*. I don't like to arouse 'public interest' with my person.

50 rue de Douai Paris
Friday morning [31 January 1879]

My dear invalid,

I was about to set off when your letter arrived. I shan't come today, as that's your wish – but I really must see you – for my sake as well as for *yours* – so I'll come on *Monday*. What do you mean about *two* hours? I'll arrive in the morning and will stay until the following day. If you have no bed to give me, I'll go and sleep in Rouen. As it is more than possible that I shall set off for Russia in a week's time, I absolutely must see you beforehand.

Why didn't you answer my telegramme (reply paid)? You kept me in a state of real anxiety for a whole day! And Mme Viardot as well, who asks me to tell you that she did not know herself until that day what close feelings she had for you. I wrote to Mme Commanville yesterday morning and her reply calmed my fears. However she spoke only of a sprain, and I see you have none the less broken your leg. I had a dream where you showed me the exact spot – just below the right knee.

So – until *Monday* – *'te volente aut nolente'*![11] I shall have a lot of things to tell you, and a lot of things to listen to.

I hope that you'll be completely fit when I get back from Russia, which will be in six weeks' time. In the meantime I embrace you.

Your
Iv. Turgenev

[Croisset]

Wednesday 5 o'clock [5 February 1879]

Thank you for your telegramme, my dear friend. I have just sent you another one, which you will receive before this note.

I have put stupid pride aside, and I accept. For above all, one must avoid dying of hunger, which is a stupid way to die.

Now I would like to know what will come of it, and if I can *count* on this situation. I fear that Ferry[12] may have his own protégés and that, when it comes out into the open, rivals will spoil my chances. Before you leave, try to find out for me what I can be certain of.

I wish you were already back from Russia. Your visit was balm. Besides I owe my judicious decision to your tender eloquence.

I embrace you as I love you, that is with all my strength.

Your old

G. Flaubert

50 rue de Douai Paris
Friday morning [7 February 1879]

My dear friend,

Here is my answer to your two letters: be reassured – we are working on your affair – and I must say that Zola and the Charpentiers are being *very good* about it. I am very glad that you consent, and I *shan't leave* for Russia until it's sorted out. I'll keep you informed. There is a little snag that has come up: Baudry is Sénard's son-in-law, and Sénard took part in the formation of the new government. But Gambetta continues to show a lively interest in you – and that's the main thing. We'll do all that's necessary.

You say nothing of your foot – that's a good sign. I hope so at least. My greetings to good M. Laporte.[13]

I embrace you.

I. Turgenev

P.S.   I'll probably write to you tomorrow.

[Croisset]
Saturday night [8 February 1879]

My good dear old fellow,

I do not thank you for the trouble you are going to on my account, that would be an insult; but it upsets me to know that you are putting off your journey to Russia because of this affair.

More than ever I am determined not to sacrifice myself for the sake of the excellent M. Baudry. So let my friends go into action! You know I am on very good terms with Mme Adam,[14] Gambetta's friend, and with Mme Pelouze, Grévy's[15] friend. If these two angels were made to speak, I doubt not that they would put in a word for me.

This morning I ordered myself a pair of crutches, that I shall try out

on Tuesday. Laporte left on Wednesday evening, but is coming back
tomorrow.

I embrace you.

Your

G. Flaubert

50 rue de Douai Paris

Sunday morning [9 February 1879]

My dear friend,

Nothing new again today; it's tomorrow that we'll get Gambetta's
final answer. I'm staying here until Thursday. I'll take great account of
the information you give me in your letter of today. I don't know
Mme Pelouze, but I think the Charpentiers know her; as for Mme
Adam, I saw her once at a sale, and she spoke to me very pleasantly. I'll
write to her to ask for an appointment. Why don't you, for your part,
write to Mme Pelouze? Now that you've made your mind up, we
must press on with it. The stupid thing about all this is that M. de
Sacy[16] is better and there's even talk of a possible recovery!

I'm pleased to know that you're going to get up on Tuesday. Mind
you don't tire your foot. I'll write to you every day until I leave.

I embrace you.

Your

I. Turgenev

[Croisset]

Monday [10 February 1879]

If I could write properly in my bed, I should explain to you why I can't
approach Mme Pelouze directly.[17] To get her to speak, fine. But to ask
her something myself, no.

You'll see, old Sacy will get better, or if he doesn't, the situation
won't be for me. I am pursued by ill fortune.

Whom shall I write to about it when you've gone?

Today my nerves are all on edge as a result of longstanding
insomnia. I only have strength enough to embrace you tenderly, my
good dear old fellow.

Yours

G. Flaubert

[Croisset]
Thursday morning 11 o'clock [13 February 1879]

My dear old fellow,
Now that you have won me over, I really *want* that post, the very idea of which made me indignant; and as I want it, I think I shan't get it.
Old de Sacy is perhaps already dead, according to what I see in *Le Temps*. There'll be a scuffle to take his place. Will Gambetta think of me? Ferry may already have given it to someone else. It'll be decided very soon.
Who will *keep an eye open* while you're away? Who will go and see Gambetta straightaway and sew the thing up?
A note in answer before you leave, please? And thank you again. I embrace you.

Your
G. Flaubert

[Telegramme]   Paris
13 February 1879

Gustave Flaubert at Croisset near Rouen.
Give up all hope, definitive refusal, letter gives details.
Turgenev

50 rue de Douai Paris
Thursday morning [13 February 1879]

My dear friend,
You already know, from my telegramme this morning of the collapse of all our plans. Here are the details. On my return to Paris, we had taken the following decisions: I was to try and speak to Gambetta, then to Ferry, and if necessary to Baudry. Thursday evening – first letter from Zola (enclosed) – and then a lull. I requested an interview of Mme Ed. Adam; no answer. Monday morning – a letter from Zola accompanying a note from Mme Charpentier (I enclose them as well). You can imagine my amazement. I took a carriage and went straight to the presidential palace to see Gambetta (the Charpentiers had promised to have a definite answer by *Saturday*). I am not received, but I see his private secretary M. Arnauld (son of Mme Arnauld of the Ariège). I explain the whole business to him: he listens to me with good grace, while wriggling about on the spot – he

makes some notes on a piece of paper – and makes the solemn promise to send a reply the very next morning. Naturally nothing comes. I take myself off to see his mother, whom I had recently met: a poker face. I return home, write a letter to Gambetta – and take it that very evening to Mme Arnauld asking her to have my letter passed on by her son. I add that I will come to her house for the answer the following day. The following day, that is yesterday, Wednesday, I return to Mme Arnauld's: nothing! – at the same time I receive a letter from Mme Edmond Adam who they said was in Cannes (I enclose that also). I put on my suit, white tie – and there I am in her drawing-room, where I find just about all of the political notables and from where France is governed and administered. I am very well received by her – I explain the matter to her . . . 'But Gambetta is here – he's having an after-dinner smoke – we shall know all directly.' She comes back two minutes later: 'Impossible my dear sir! Gambetta has already got people in mind.' The dictator arrives with measured step: I've never seen trained dogs dance around their master like the ministers and senators etc. surrounding him. He starts to talk to one of them. Mme Ed. Adam takes me by the hand and leads me to him; but the great man declines the honour of making my acquaintance – and repeats – loud enough for me to hear: 'I don't want it – it's been said – it's impossible.' I make myself scarce, and return home, *plunged*, as they say, in thoughts that I don't need to tell you. And that's how much one can trust fine words and promises.

The two positions that Mme Charpentier mentions will go to MM. Baudry and Soury.

Come my good fellow – we must throw all that overboard – and get back to work, literary work, the only thing worthy of a man such as you. I'm not leaving until *Saturday* (at 7 o'clock in the morning). You *have* time to write to me. Let me have news of you – can you walk on your crutches now?

I'll write to you from Moscow.

I embrace you very strongly.

Your
Iv. Turgenev[18]

P.S.   I'm sending a note to your niece.

Paris
Thursday [13 February 1879]

My dear friend,

I have just seen Zola to whom I have told everything and who, through affection for you (this lad is very fond of you I know), is sorry that I told you the whole truth. He didn't want you to give up all hope of it straightaway. (N.B.   Mme Ed. Adam promised me to 'work' on your behalf during my absence, accompanying those words with strong phrases saying that France owed it to you etc. I didn't mention it in my letter.) All in all – I think I owed you the whole truth; the instinct of friendship drove me to it. However I'm giving you Zola's opinion. N.B.   I didn't tell him I'd sent you the supporting evidence – his letters – and perhaps you'd do well not to mention them. It is clear that your friends did everything they could; but it's probable that they were mistaken in the benevolent intentions they presumed on.

I hope you won't think that these difficulties have upset me personally: I was very sorry that our actions led only to a fiasco – for your sake; as for the contact with the high and mighty of the day I would almost say that I found it amusing – for I got quite a good inside view of things.

Come now – let's say no more about it – and let me embrace you again.

> Your
> Iv. Turgenev

> [Croisset]
> Friday 5 o'clock [14 February 1879]

My dear old fellow,

I mourn the loss without much effort; and deep down (you'll recognise me there, you who are a psychologist) I'm *perhaps* not sorry.

Moreover the emoluments are mediocre, the situation, obliging me to stay longer in Paris, would only have made me even more hard up; for I live better and more cheaply at Croisset than in the capital. So as long as I don't get a real *sinecure* giving me about six thousand francs at least, it's better to stay as I am. Tell our friends the Charpentiers and Zola, whose behaviour touches me. Would it be a good idea for me to write to them? And to Mme Adam? (That's more difficult.)

I would have been sorry, if, in your zeal, you had gone to see Baudry, who is behaving towards me like a real swine. Being perfectly free with him, I can at least tell him what I think of him. However he must know that people were acting on my behalf. Anyway I don't care. If he talks to me about it, I'll blame my friends; and then it's everyone for himself.

I won't say anything to Zola about your sending the dossier.

So, my good old fellow, *an immediate end to all intrigue*, until your return. That's an order.

I'm afraid that Mme Adam will meddle while you're away, and that one of these days I'll be offered a derisory post that I should refuse. Then I should appear ungrateful and ill-tempered. How can that be avoided? I'll leave you to judge as to the means. But you must be very busy with preparations for your departure. Let me have news of you often, or ask Mme Viardot on my behalf to let me know when she hears from you. The plague will worry me, I'm like that.[19]

As my gumboot was hurting me horribly, they split it for me from top to bottom, then bound it with tape; and as far as the leg is concerned, it's fine. But I'm very weak and the state of my nerves is bad. Without having the slightest spot on my skin, I scratch myself all night and I barely sleep. I need to take baths, which is impossible. My greatest relief is not to be using the *bedpan* any more!

I daren't ask you to write to me again before you leave. However? . . .

Come, farewell. Look after yourself and come back quickly.

I give you a big hug.

Your old

G. Flaubert

A native of Rouen, Senator Cordier, whom I'm on close terms with, came to see me on Monday. As he gets on well with Ferry I'd asked him to speak to him. I'll write and tell him not to bother.

50 rue de Douai Paris
Saturday morning [15 February 1879]

My dear friend,

I'm leaving in an hour and I only have time to tell you how pleased I am at the way in which you're taking all this. You would do well to drop a line to Charpentier and to Zola. As for Mme Adam, it's perhaps better to keep quiet.

We'll see when I get back in 5 or 6 weeks' time. Perhaps you'll already be in Paris by then.

I'll write to you from *Moscow*. In the meantime I embrace you.

Your

I.T.

St Petersburg Hotel 31 U.D. Linden Berlin
Tuesday 18 February 79

My dear friend,

You can imagine the annoyance caused me by the *Figaro* article[20] – which I only found out about on Sunday, on the railway journey, at

I've forgotten which station? This annoyance was all the greater for knowing that you would be feeling it also. I'll go to the devil if I know who this M. Aristophanes can be. My visit to Mme E.A. was on Wednesday evening – and I didn't leave the house on Thursday or Friday, thanks to a bad head cold – and on Saturday I left for Russia. I only spoke of this affair to Viardot and his wife, and to Zola; they're not the kind to write to the *Figaro*. Anyway fate has decreed that everything will go wrong in this business.

I've been here since yesterday evening, I'm leaving today for Petersburg, where I expect to arrive the day after tomorrow. On Sunday I'll be in Moscow, and on Monday or Tuesday I'll write to you.

In the meantime keep well – that is walk without crutches – and don't be cross with me. I embrace you.

Your

Iv. Turgenev

[Croisset]
Monday 7 [April 1879]

My good dear old fellow,

I read in *Le Temps* of Sunday (yesterday) that M. Turgenev is back in Paris.

I need to embrace you. When are you coming? (According to your promise in February.) We shall have a lot to rattle on about!

My niece, who has spent the week with me, left just an hour ago. I was awaiting her departure to tell Zola and Charpentier that they may make their visit now. But as I put yours above all other, I'm waiting for a note from you to *assign* them a day. Who's stopping you from coming straightaway? In any case, a note, please?

I embrace you.

Your old lame

G. Flaubert

Yesterday I had one of my last teeth out, and today I have bad backache, lumbago.

[Croisset]
Tuesday 3 o'clock [*sic* for Wednesday] [9 April 1879]

Our two letters crossed my good dear old fellow. I shan't be able to go to Paris for *a month or six weeks*. To wait to see you until then would be a long time.

Tell me when I may have at last the pleasure of embracing my good Turgenev, because after your visit I'll write to Zola and Charpentier to come and lunch at Croisset.

Arrange things i) to stay under my roof for some time: we have an infinite amount to talk about! And ii) I have three chapters to read to you.

Until then I embrace you.

> Your
>
> G. Flaubert

Popelin wrote to me this morning that my niece's portrait of M. Cloquet has been accepted.[21] So much the better. My thanks to Viardot.

> 50 rue de Douai Paris
> Saturday morning [26 April 1879]

My dear old fellow,

You are certainly going to call me a soggy pear, a wet rag, spineless creature etc. – and I add that you are right. However, listen *before* you hit me. (This is what distinguishes me from Themistocoles.) Everyone here is leaving today – and I would have been free – *but* Paul Viardot is giving his concert tomorrow (which I had forgotten) and I can't miss going to it. On Tuesday evening I have to give a reading (to our Society for the Protection of Russian Artists) for charitable purposes! So I could come on Wednesday . . . *but* at a Sardanapalian dinner that Zola gave us the day before yesterday – it was arranged that he, Daudet, Goncourt and me, would come and see you on *Sunday* (not tomorrow, a week later) – we'll arrive for lunch, they would leave in the evening, and I'll stay with you for the whole of Monday. Now, as you have the right to trust me no longer, I submit myself to your invectives with good grace . . .

But I think it will come off this time!

And on this I embrace you and remain your

> Iv. Turgenev

> [Croisset]
> Sunday morning [27 April 1879]

No, I won't pour invective down upon you; but if you knew the *nervous upset* that you cause me, you would feel remorse. I spare you the curses of my cook.

Your reasons seem absurd my dear friend. It seems to me that young Viardot can play the violin without you, and that your company is not indispensable to him.

Frankly, your disagreeableness is as great as the affection that I feel for you, which is saying a great deal. You promise a visit for months on end; you *Always* break your word; then, barely arrived, when one thinks one has got hold of you, you leave again very soon. No! No! It's not kind.

I don't know what was decided at Zola's Sardanapalian dinner. But my good fellow, as my entire livery consists of one single servant, a woman, she can't prepare and serve a lunch for six. I *have* (!!!!) to receive my friends one at a time, and not all together.

And what! Haven't you understood, my dear good old fellow, that my happiness would be spoilt if I saw you arriving with others. One doesn't show one's . . . in public, by God! But you are a man who likes social occasions – all the vices.

In short, do as you wish. Come when you're free of all obligations, and don't torment me any more by promising joys that are not fulfilled.

Thereupon, my good fellow, I embrace you.
                    Your old wounded
                                                    G. Flaubert

                                        50 rue de Douai Paris
                                        [7 May 1879]

My dear old fellow,
    The 'sprotten' won't arrive for a week yet;[22] in the meantime I've sent you some other Swedish fish which are nothing like as good as 'sprotten'. Two pounds are being sent today – and I shall see your niece today. The 3 chapters you read to me gave me the greatest pleasure, especially the 2nd and the 3rd. Work hard, cheer yourself up, and come here as soon as you can.

    In the meantime – I am also going to try to work, and I embrace you.
                                        Your
                                        Iv. Turgenev

                                        [Croisset]
                    Thursday morning [8 May 1879][23]

I received the two boxes today, my dear old fellow. One of them is even half-eaten. Thank you for the present. Thank you even more for the thirty-six hours spent with me. Your departure left me very sad. 'Things are not going well.' I feel deeply stricken. There is too little pleasure in my life. And as for my book, it is weighing me down. The result, whatever it is, will not repay the effort.

Love me always, my dear great man. I embrace you affectionately.

Your

G. Flaubert

50 rue de Douai Paris
Sunday morning [25 May 1879]

My dear old fellow,

I need to have news of you. Let me know i) if you have *anything* to say to me? Has there been any improvement in your affairs? ii) How is your health? Your work? iii) Are you coming to Paris and when? As from Friday I shall be at Bougival. I have a room I can offer you there. The air is good and there are large sofas on which one can stretch out full length. But write quickly.

In the meantime I embrace you.

Your

Iv. Turgenev

[Croisset]
Monday 26 [May 1879]

My good dear old fellow,

Unless the world comes to an end next week, you will see me in the middle of the said week. As soon as I'm in Paris, there will be a note from me to let you know.

I'm finishing *B. and P.*'s *Magic* and I'm exhausted by it.

I embrace you vigorously.

Your

G. Flaubert

240 rue du Faubourg St Honoré [Paris]
Monday 2 June [1879]

My old darling,

Here I am, having arrived yesterday evening. How to arrange a meeting? I fully intend to go to Bougival, but not straightaway, as I am already weighed down with errands and appointments. I'm dining in town every evening this week.

Is there a day when you come into Paris? I daren't arrange an appointment, through fear of not being able to keep it. I normally come back towards three or four o'clock to rest my legs. You would have a chance of finding me at that hour.

Next Sunday I shan't shift the whole day. So I'm counting on you then, at the latest. Until then I embrace you.

Your

G. Flaubert

[Paris]

[5 June 1879]

Gustave Flaubert, 240 Faubourg St Honoré, Paris.
Sunday for sure, will call tomorrow at about four.
Turgenev

Les Frenes Bougival

Friday evening 13 June 79

My good old fellow,

I'm probably leaving for London tomorrow evening. In any case, I shall not be able to dine with you, and I put off this great pleasure until after my return which will be in a week's time. Don't scold me too much – and when I explain it all to you, you won't be cross with me.[24] In the meantime I embrace you.

Your

Iv. Turgenev

P.S.   It seems to me that there is a change for the better in your affairs
– I'm *very glad about it.*
P.S.   If I don't leave on Saturday I'll come and see you on Sunday.

The Chalet Les Frenes Bougival (Seine-et-Oise)

Thursday 7 August 79

My dear friend,

Decidedly it is too long since I heard from you. Write two lines about what you're doing, how you are etc., etc. As for me, I'm physically very well; but as for the state of my *soul* – you can get a very accurate idea by lifting up the lid of a cesspool and looking in; moreover it should not be an English 'water-closet': they are generally clean.

All my little world here send you their best wishes; I do also – from the depths of my *spleen* – for you know I love you dearly.

Your

Iv. Turgenev

[Croisset]
Saturday 6 p.m. [9 August 1879]

Ah, at last! I have news of you, my dear good old fellow! So you are very fed up – but I prefer the *lavatorial* state of your soul to the gouty state of your body.

Perhaps your moral sufferings come from your Doctoral mortarboard? Or from the fact that you haven't had the opportunity to break your word to me? I'm still awaiting an explanation for your last piece of treachery, for you were supposed to dine at my place one Saturday in the month of June. Since then, no sign of the fellow!

As for me, *B. and P.* are wearing me out. I have only four pages to go to finish the Philosophy chapter. After which I shall start the penultimate chapter. These last two will take me up to March or April. Then there'll be the second volume! In short I shall still be at it in a year's time. One needs to be a master of asceticism to inflict such labours on oneself! On certain days it seems to me that all the blood is drained from my limbs and that my death is imminent. Then I bounce back, and things are all right *all the same*. There you are.

You will be pleased to learn that there is a little blue sky on the financial horizon of my life. Commanville has managed to set up a sawmill again. He is launched anew. Provided he doesn't sink again! But I don't think so: the business seems to me a good one.

My niece isn't very well. She is anaemic and subject to almost constant migraines.

No news from our friends.

If you are in Paris towards the middle of September, I hope to see you there when I'm at Saint-Gratien at the princess's.

You don't seem very busy. *So,* there's nothing to stop you writing me a long letter. Do it, it would be a charitable act.

Friendly greetings and my respects to all at your place. I embrace you tenderly.

Your old

G. Flaubert

[Croisset]
Tuesday [26 August 1879]

My good fellow,
It's Mme Régnier's fault. She insisted to Caroline that you had been decorated for bravery, whereas you have simply been honoured with a university title.[25] What irony!
I know indirectly through Maupassant that you are well.
I shall be in Paris on Thursday evening at about 5 o'clock. Would you like to come and call for me between 5 and 6 to dine with me and Sir Guy or to lunch on Friday morning? At the moment I can't offer you any other day.
A note of reply to me in Paris, please, so that I shall have it on my arrival.
Try to come on Thursday. Until then I embrace you.
Your old
G. Flaubert

[Paris]
Friday evening [29 August 1879]

My good old fellow,
In a few days' time, when I'm back in Paris, I'll write to you and we'll try and meet up, damn it all!
Maupassant told me that you were getting ready to seek out *the silence of the study* in the depths of Russia. I find that astounding!
Mme Adam warned me in a letter that I found on my table yesterday evening, and just now in person, that I should have a work of yours to correct. How much truth is there in all this?
G. Flaubert

The Chalet Les Frenes Bougival Seine-et-Oise
Saturday 30 August 79

My good old fellow,
It's agreed, and I shall await your signal to come running.
I am in fact planning to go to Russia – not to work – indeed! – but quite simply to breathe in my native air (as the inhabitants of Marseilles would say). This decision has got me out of the nervous frustration which was devouring me, to put it pompously. Laugh if you like – but the idea of plunging into this quagmire up to my neck has calmed me

down. 'What a thing human nature is!' to revert to the same pompous tone.

I had to promise a little story of 10 pages to Mme Adam – and I took the liberty of telling her that I was counting on submitting this major work to you for checking.[26] There – you've been warned and towards the end of November I shall descend upon you with my manuscript!

I also am impatient to get to know *B. and P.*'s philosophy. It all depends on you. I await and while waiting I embrace you.

Your
Iv. Turgenev

P.S.   I have read the first episodes of Daudet's novel?????[27]

[Paris]
Thursday 11 September [1879]

My old darling,

Answer the following question for me *straightaway*: would you like, next Monday, to come and collect me at my place at about eleven o'clock? We will lunch together, then I'll read you my chapter. After which I shall leave for Saint-Gratien, where I must be at about five o'clock. If you can't manage Monday, what about dinner on Saturday? (Saturday week.) But it's next Monday that would suit me best.

Your
G. Flaubert

The Chalet Les Frenes Bougival (Seine-et-Oise)
Thursday 6 November 79

Let's see, my good old fellow, I must write to you and find out what you're up to. As for me, I haven't moved from here, and things have not been going too well so far. Mme Viardot's second daughter has given birth – rather painfully – to a little girl – a month ago now – and mother and baby are well; but her eldest daughter (Jeanne) has caught scarlet fever – she's been in quarantine for 3 weeks now, and it will be as long again. Marianne has a bad attack of the 'flu and can't go out. M. and Mme Viardot have been back in Paris since Monday – and I stay here like an old oyster that doesn't even open with the sun. My heart is giving me cause for anxiety with palpitations, night cramps etc.

I have finished the translation of the little article for Mme Adam's journal, and I'll send it to you, or I'll bring it to you, so that you can make the necessary corrections. I'll let you know beforehand and I thank you in advance. The thing is very short.

I don't think I've ever read anything as perfectly *boring* as 'Nana' (this between ourselves).[28] It is so down-to-earth and painstaking that one almost dies of it; and the few coarse words in it, that are like peppercorns, are not enough to give flavour to this insipid porridge. It seems also that the general opinion is that it's a flop.

I embrace you – I'll see you soon in any case.

Your
I. Turgenev

[Croisset]
[8 November 1879]

My old darling,

Send me, or better bring me your work when you like. Don't make any promises, don't tell me you're coming. Warn me twenty-four hours in advance, and *come*, that's all I ask you.

B. *and P.*, who send you their respects, are now about their devotions. They are going 'to approach the altar'; I think this chapter on Religion will make the Ecclesiastical gentlemen take a dim view of me? I have stuffed myself with pious literature! At last on New Year's Day I hope to embark on the last chapter, and when that's finished, I shall have six months' more to go.

My niece is leaving me in a week's time, and I shall be alone until the spring. This evening I shall have a visit from young Maupassant. That's all, my good fellow.

I have only read five or six episodes of *Nana*: consequently I can't talk about it. But I have delighted in Renan's new volume; what a jewel of erudition![29]

Say nice things to everyone, beginning with Mme Viardot and ending with the new-born baby.

I embrace you very tenderly.

Your old
G. Flaubert

You don't mention the gout. It's left you then? So much the better.

I also feel very old sometimes, weary, exhausted in my bones. Never mind! I carry on, and would like not to die before having emptied a few more buckets of sh— on the heads of my fellow men.

That's the only thing that keeps me going.

The Chalet Les Frenes Bougival (Seine-et-Oise)
Thursday 13 November 79

My dear good old fellow,

I shall bring the proofs of my little thing to Croisset in person. That will be towards the beginning of December, for the thing itself will come out in the edition of the 15th. You will be warmed 24 hours in advance.

Do you know what we have been reading for the last 6 days with enchantment, with delight? *Sentimental Education*! After our other readings (it's true that there were novels from the 'Revue des 2 Mondes' amongst them – and you know what that means) it seems marvellous to us! In this diamond there is however a flaw, a single one: it's the description of Mme Arnoux's *singing*: i) as one imagines her she ought to sing differently and something else, ii) a *contralto* voice cannot aim for effect in the *high* notes, the third even *higher* than the first two, iii) you should have specified musically what she is singing – without that the effect remains vague and even slightly comic. That was not your intention was it? But you remember the classic line:

'*Ubi plura nitent in carmine . . .*'[30]

I wish B. and P. the necessary contrition for their great religious act – the more intense it is, the more vigorously they'll rebel against it afterwards.

My health is good – my gout remains quiet, but there are still invalids in the house. I conveyed your greetings to the Viardots, and they thank you for them.

I give you a friendly embrace.

Your

Iv. Turgenev

[Croisset]
Wednesday 19 [November 1879]

My old darling,

Undoubtedly the passage in question is not brilliant. I even find it a bit silly. However a contralto voice can reach high notes, witness Alboni;[31] and basically I think you're being hard. Note, in mitigation, that my hero is not a musician and that my heroine is a very middling sort of person. None the less, between you and me this paragraph has always worried me. While writing it, I must have been troubled by contradictory memories.

I am very pleased at the impression that *Sentimental Education* is creating. Without committing the sin of pride, I consider that this book has been judged wrongly, its ending especially. I bear a grudge against the reading public for that.

What would be nice – since you announce a visit in the month of December, would be to come on the 12th, anniversary of my birth. We would celebrate, or rather lament together this event – hardly worthy of note.

My niece has been in Paris since Sunday, and this is the beginning of my solitude. I am halfway with my Religion now. What a burden that book is, my dear friend!

I read avidly the story of your nihilist in *Le Temps*.[32] Oh Jesus, is it possible to make living creatures suffer so atrociously!

Mme Adam has written asking me to be a patron of the flood victims of Murcia. I ask for nothing better; but what will it involve? So far she has not answered this question.

I have heard that *Nana* has not had much success on the whole. Is it true?

When you have nothing better to do, write to your

G. Flaubert who holds you dear and embraces you.

Les Frenes Bougival
Sunday 23 November 79

My good old fellow,

Certainly I'll come to Croisset on the 12th – with two bottles of champagne under my arm, to celebrate the howmanyeth year of your existence? Just two weeks ago – on 9 November – I was 61!

You will have the proofs of my thing for 'La Nouvelle Revue' in the first days of December, and correct them harshly, if you find something that's not quite right.

I am, like you, a patron of the reception in aid of the flood victims of Murcia. (The date of the reception is set for 11 November [*sic*].) All that we shall have to do (for I assume you'll accept) is to put on a suit, a white tie, and *honour* the party with our presence, with a little badge in our buttonhole. You see it's not difficult. You would have to send your acceptance and then come to Paris on the 11th or the evening of the 10th – and we would leave together for Croisset on the evening of the 11th or the 12th first thing in the morning. There you are!

We are continuing to read 'Sentimental Education' *en famille* and still with the same pleasure.

No, 'Nana' has had no success. There were, however, two quite fine chapters a few days ago. But on the whole, it's boring – and what would displease Zola especially, it is as naive as can be, and tendancious (Is that the right spelling?) to the devil!

I have an engagement with your niece tomorrow. I'm leaving the country at the end of this week.

I shall see you again soon – I embrace you.

Your

Iv. Turgenev

[Croisset]

Tuesday 2 December [1879]

Just a line.

Mme Adam writes that she's going to send me the proofs of your work, and that I shall have to send it back to her straightaway. That's not right is it? To you first. And then it seems to me that we can talk about it much better face to face than by letter. So bring me the thing on the 12th of this month, a week on Friday.

B. and P. are wearing me out. Frankly I can't take any more.

I have enough strength left to embrace you. I shall see you soon.

Your old

G. Flaubert

50 rue de Douai Paris

Tuesday 2 December 79

Here is, my good old fellow, the task I told you about and which falls to you. And this is what I ask of your goodwill. Read this little piece of silliness, correct, change, cut out what you will – and send it back tomorrow if possible! I shall be grateful to you, as much as one can possibly be.

I have been back in Paris for two days. You didn't say whether you approved of my plan – for you – to come here on the 11th? In any case I'll spend the day of the 12th at Croisset. That matter is settled.

A thousand thanks in advance – and I embrace you.

Iv. Turgenev

[Croisset]

Wednesday 5 o'clock [3 December 1879]

You will receive your *parcel* at the same time as this. Included is a little note of explanation.

No, I shan't go to Paris for the Spaniards, it would be too silly. But I expect you on the 12th.

B. and P. are not coming on very well. The weather is making me sad, and I'm worn out by my reading. But thank God that's finished!
I embrace you.

> Your old
> G. Flaubert

[Croisset]
Monday evening 8 December [1879]

It's agreed, settled and sworn on, and don't let me down by God! It would be a cruel thing. So on Friday next, the 12th of this month, I expect you for dinner.

And arrange things so that you can stay until Monday. Be so good, *I beg you.* We have so much to talk about, and I am so virtuous that I deserve much kindness.

Until then, I embrace you.

> Your old
> G. Flaubert

[Croisset]
Friday 26 December [1879]

Generous man,

I have not yet received the caviar or the salmon. By what means did you dispatch these two boxes? My stomach is ravaged with anxiety.

Your journey to Russia upsets me extraordinarily, my poor old fellow. It seems to me that this departure is more significant than the others. Why? Do you really need to go, is it unavoidable? Arrange things so as to avoid a long absence, and come back quickly to France where your friends and loved ones are.

I am now preparing the last eight pages of my Religion. I am afraid that that chapter will be rather dry.

I embrace you strongly.

> Your
> G. Flaubert

50 rue de Douai Paris
Saturday morning [27 December 1879]

My good old fellow,

The caviar and the salmon were sent *4 days* ago 'care of *M. Pilon,* quai du Havre, Rouen – to be handed to M. G.F.' (This address was given to me by Commanville.) Find out what you can. I should be particularly sorry if the salmon were to be lost, it was splendid.

This cold spell is freezing me – and reducing me to stupidity. However I have started preparations for my departure. 'The wine (what a wine!!) has been opened – it must be drunk.'

I shall send you shortly a novel in 3 vols by Count Leo Tolstoy, whom I consider to be the foremost contemporary writer. You know who in my opinion could challenge him in that position. Unfortunately it has been translated by a Russian lady . . . and in general I am apprehensive about lady translators, especially when it's such a vigorous writer as Tolstoy is.

In the meantime I embrace you.

Your
I.T.

[Croisset]
Sunday evening [28 December 1879]

I received the box yesterday evening. The salmon is magnificent, but the caviar makes me cry out in ecstasy. When shall we eat such things together? I wish you were gone and come back. Write to me at least from over there.

It looks like thawing this evening. Can it be true?

As for Tolstoy's novel, have it sent to my niece's. Commanville will bring it to me.

All the best, my dear old fellow. Your old fellow embraces you.

G. Flaubert

[Croisset]
Tuesday evening [30 December 1879]

Thank you! Many, many thanks, oh Saint Vincent de Paul of gastronomy! My word, you are treating me like a kept man! Too many delicacies! Well I must tell you that I'm eating the caviar almost without bread, like jam.

As for the novel, its three volumes frighten me. Three volumes unconnected with my work are hard going now. Never mind, I shall tackle it. As I expect to have finished my chapter towards the end of next week (!!!!) it will be a relaxation before starting the next.

When are you leaving, or rather when are you coming back? It's stupid to love one another as we do and to see so little of each other. I embrace you.

Your old

G. Flaubert

[Croisset]

[January 1880]

My dear friend,

Last summer Mme Viardot and all her family told me how much they liked cider.

So I take the liberty of making them a present of a barrel that comes from Croisset.

Emile, who is accompanying the said beverage, will tell you what to do with it.

How are you? I am not so well: I feel ill, but cannot locate it to any particular organ, and I'm sad enough to die.

I embrace you.

G. Flaubert

[Croisset]

Wednesday evening [21 January 1880]

Just two lines, my good dear old fellow. i) When are you leaving, or rather no: when are you coming back? Are you less worried about the consequences of your journey? ii) Thank you for making me read Tolstoy's novel. It's first rate. What a painter and what a psychologist! The first two are sublime; but the third goes terribly to pieces. He repeats himself and he philosophises! In fact the man, the author, the Russian are visible, whereas up until then one had seen only Nature and Humanity. It seems to me that in places he has some elements of Shakespeare. I uttered cries of admiration during my reading of it . . . and it's long! Tell me about the *author*. Is it his first book? In any case he has his head *well screwed on*! Yes! It's very good! Very good!

I've finished my *Religion* and I'm working on the plan of my last chapter: *Education*.

My niece came to spend three full days here. She left this morning, and she bemoans that fact that our dear friend the great Turgenev is abandoning us. I embrace you tenderly.

Your old

G. Flaubert

50 rue de Douai Paris
Saturday 24 January 80

My good old fellow,
You cannot imagine the pleasure your letter gave me and what you say about Tolstoy's novel. Your approval confirms my own ideas about him. Yes, he is a man of great talent, and yet you put your finger on the weak spot: he also has built himself a philosophical system, which is at one and the same time mystical, childish and presumptuous, and whic has spoilt his third volume dreadfully, and the second novel that he wrote after 'War and Peace' – and where there are also things of the first order. I don't know what the critics will say. (I have sent 'War and Peace' to Daudet and Zola as well.) But for me the matter is settled: *Flaubertus dixit*. The rest is of no significance.
I am pleased to see that your old fellows are coming along.
I'll be leaving Paris in the course of next week, but I'll write you a note before I go. In the meantime I embrace you.

Your

Iv. Turgenev

Croisset near Deville (Seine-Inférieure)
Thursday 4 March [1880]

My old darling,
As you no longer write to me once you are in Russia, the correspondence between me and Mme Viardot has started up again.
A letter from her informs me that you have sciatica, that you are sad, that you are fed up etc. and she exhorts me to write to you to cheer you up. Why can I not, my poor old fellow, send you all the flowers of the world and of life?
What can I tell you? That Du Camp has been elected to the Académie Française! That you surely knew? It makes me giddy . . . Why 'court this honour'? How ridiculous men are!
I have started my last chapter and I've got to page seven. There will be forty. When shall I have finished it? God only knows. Whatever happens, I plan to spend the months of May and June in Paris, then I shall return by [September] and will not budge for a long time. So we shall see each other!   ?
I've read *Nana* in volume form, in one sitting, and I think you're a bit hard on it. There are some fine things, superb cries of passion and two or three characters (that of Mignon amongst others) that delighted me.
Young Maupassant narrowly escaped a libel suit. I say escaped, as

the proceedings, which had barely begun, were dropped. I published a letter on the subject in *Le Gaulois* (the last Saturday of February) and I didn't even have time to read through my piece! Consequently it's quite badly put together. I've never made such a concession to any one, but the poor young devil moved me to pity. I must say (strictly *between you and me*) that my disciple's health worries me. His *heart* will play a nasty trick on him one of these days, I fear.

Have you thought about Commanville's business, seeing a lawyer about the woods of Prince Solloouh? (That can't be the spelling? Never mind.)

In your friendship for me, you'll be pleased to learn that there is now some blue sky on my financial horizon. Commanville has got a sawmill going again, he has found some funds. The contract should be signed, perhaps, this evening? Once that's done, Commanville is leaving for Odessa immediately.

My niece, alone in Paris, is hastening to finish a portrait for the Exhibition. You know she is not at all pleased with you, and I'm sure she'll speak ill of you this evening at Mme Viardot's.

What else? A pile of little books sent to me by young writers that it's not worth naming. *Conscience* makes me read them, and that makes me waste time, and so I get cross! I already have so much to read for *B. and P.* now I am lost in education systems, including ways of preventing masturbation! Important issue! The further I get, the more ridiculous I find the significance attached to the uro-genital organs. It's time we laughed at them – not at the organs, but at those people who want to base the whole of human morality on them.

Today the weather is splendid, the shrubs are in bud, and the violets are poking through the lawn. So you can imagine your friend in his setting. Yours is misty and uncertain for me . . .

So come back to us, and write me as long a letter as you can.

From the bottom of my heart and with arms outstretched,

your old

G. Flaubert

[Croisset]
Wednesday 7 April [1880]

My good dear old fellow,

I rejoice in the thought that I shall see you again in about a month. All the worries you had have disappeared, thank God! And soon we shall be able to talk about them at length.

Were your ears burning on Easter Sunday? Here we drank a toast to Turgenev and regretted his absence. Those who clinked their champagne glasses to your health were: (i) your humble servant, then Zola, Charpentier, A. Daudet, Goncourt, Fortin my doctor and 'that little rascal Maupassant' as Lagier says. On the subject of Maupassant, he's not in such a bad way as I feared; he has nothing organically wrong, but this young man has chronic gout, is ultra-rheumatic and is a complete nervous wreck. After dining here these gentlemen spent the night and left the following day after lunch. I had a job to stop myself reading something from *B. and P.* to them.

When Pradier was working at the Invalides in 1848, he used to say 'The Emperor's tomb will become my own',[33] so weary was he with the task. And I can say it's time my book were finished, otherwise I shall be. Frankly it's driving me mad, and I'm exhausted by it. It's becoming a chore! And I've still got three months to go without counting the second volume which will take me six! All in all I'm afraid that the result won't have been worth the effort that has gone into it, and I feel so worn out that the ending could well be insipid and a flop. Moreover, I no longer understand any of it, and my limbs feel as if they've taken a thrashing, I have stomach cramps and I barely sleep these days. But that's enough moaning!

This is how I plan my existence: I hope to be in Paris towards 10 May and to stay there until the end of June, to spend two months at Croisset making Extracts for my second volume, then to return to Paris in September and to stay for a long time.

Commanville should be in Trieste today. He is pleased with his journey to Russia. My niece, whose two pictures have been accepted for the Exhibition sends you her greetings.

The newspapers have slung mud at our friend Du Camp, the new member of the Academy.

La Vie Moderne continues to disgrace me with the illustrations for *Le Château des Coeurs*. My poor fairy play has had no luck. But then why did I listen to the advice of Other People? Why did I give in!

I read none of the books that are sent to me, consequently I can give you no literary news.

I am now principally indignant against Botanists.[34] It is impossible to get them to understand a question that seems as clear as anything to me! You'll see for yourself, and you will be amazed at how small the faculty of judgement is in these brains.

Try to find a few minutes to write to me. That would be kind. Don't delay your return to us.

I embrace you with open arms, my dear old fellow.

Your

G. Flaubert

[Croisset]
Thursday 15 April [1880]

My old darling,

N.B.   Commanville begs you to send him the name and address of your lawyer; so that he may, on your recommendation, get in touch with him. He (Commanville) came back from Russia last Saturday, delighted with the business he has done there. His sawmill will be working in less than two months.

As for me, my good fellow, I am exhausted. *B. and P.* are getting me down, and it's time it were finished; otherwise I shall be finished myself.

My intention is to be in Paris towards 8 or 10 May, probably three weeks from next Sunday. My first volume won't be finished before the end of June. After which I'll have another six months to go.

When shall I see you again? It'll be in the middle of May won't it? How I'm longing to embrace you!

Your old
G. Flaubert

You should have received a letter from me two weeks ago.

Prechistensky boulevard Moscow
Thursday 6 May 1880

My good old fellow,

This isn't a letter – it's a sign of life that I'm giving. I am well and am darting about like a squirrel in a cage; I have been here for a week and I am leaving next Monday for the country. I shall spend ten days taking in the fragrance of the birch trees and listening to the *screech* of nightingales. I am returning to Moscow for the inaugural celebrations for the statue of our great poet, Pushkin. (N.B.   You will receive an invitation from the Committee! Of course you won't come, but if you send a telegramme it will be read out to the enthusiastic applause of the guests at the banquet.) And then I set off, and shall be in Paris in the first ten days of June, and I hope to embrace you heartily. Now as for the lawyer Commanville told you about, give him the following address:

Mr Victor Gaievsky, 48 Liteinaya Street, St Petersburg.

He is a distinguished man and an authority – and what's more he is lawyer to the French Embassy at St Petersburg. He has been warned by me and will do all he can to be of service to M. Commanville.

Give him my regards, also to your niece; I embrace you and I'll see you soon.

Your old
Iv. Turgenev

Notes

Abbreviations

Quotations from the letters of Flaubert are taken from the Conard edition of the *Correspondance – nouvelle édition* in nine volumes (1926–33) and the *Correspondance – supplément* in four volumes (1954). In the following notes, the abbreviations *Corresp.* and *Corresp. supp.* are used.

For Turgenev, all quotations, unless otherwise stated, are from the *Polnoe sobranie sochinenii i pisem*, published by the Soviet Academy of Sciences in twenty-eight volumes (1961–8). The Appreviations *Pol. sob. soch.* and *Pol. sob. pisem* are used.

All translations are my own.

Introduction

1   E.M. de Vogüé, *Le Roman russe* (1886), p. vii.
2   Flaubert, *Corresp.*, VII, p. 62.
3   Letters of 5 June 1872, 25 September 1873 and 22 December 1878.
4   Turgenev, *Pol. sob. pisem*, XII (ii), p. 256.
5   Flaubert, V, p. 154.
6   Flaubert, V, p. 167.
7   Flaubert, V, p. 422.
8   *Ivan Tourguénev: Lettres inédites à Pauline Viardot et à sa famille*, ed. H. Granjard and A. Zviguilsky (1972), p. 247.
9   Flaubert, VI, p. 317.
10 E. and J. Goncourt, *Journal – Mémoires de la vie littéraire*, ed. R. Ricotte, X, p. 75.
11 Goncourt, *Journal*, X, p. 80.
12 Flaubert, VII, p. 3.
13 Flaubert, VII, p. 11.
14 Flaubert, VII, p. 13.
15 Flaubert, VII, pp. 71–2.
16 Turgenev, *Pol. sob. pisem*, X, p. 225.
17 Flaubert, VII, p. 190.
18 Goncourt, XI, p. 17.
19 Goncourt, X, p. 171.
20 A. Daudet, *Trente ans de Paris*, quoted from *Oeuvres complètes*, vol. 12 (1930), p. 79.
21 Turgenev, *Pol. sob. pisem*, XI, p. 229.

22 Turgenev, XII (i), p. 99.
23 Turgenev, XI, p. 344.
24 Turgenev, XII (i), pp. 74–5 and p. 81.
25 Turgenev, XII (i), p. 100.
26 Turgenev, *Pol. sob. soch.*, XV, p. 112.
27 Flaubert, VII, p. 375.
28 I. Pavlovsky, *Souvenirs sur Tourguéneff* (1887), p. 71.
29 M. Kleman, *I.S. Turgenev perevodchik Flobera*, in G. Flober, *Sobranie sochinienii*, vol. 5 (1934).
30 Goncourt, XI, pp. 62–3.
31 Goncourt, XI, p. 89.
32 Turgenev, *Pol. sob. pisem*, XII (ii), p. 70.
33 Flaubert, VIII, p. 334.
34 Flaubert, VIII, p. 401.
35 Turgenev, *Pol. sob. pisem*, XII (ii), pp. 246–7.
36 *Lettres inédites à Pauline Viardot*, p. 297.
37 Turgenev, *Pol. sob. pisem*, XIII (i), pp. 7–11.
38 C. Digeon, *Le dernier visage de Flaubert* (1946), p. 60.
39 Turgenev, *Pol. sob. soch.*, XIV, p. 11.
40 Turgenev, *Pol. sob. pisem*, I, p. 176.
41 Turgenev, *Pol. sob. pisem*, XII (i), p. 83.
42 To Louise Colet and Gizhitsky for example (*Pol. sob. pisem*, XII (i), p. 288).
43 Flaubert, I, p. 21.
44 Flaubert, I, p. 339.
45 Turgenev, *Pol. sob. soch.*, X, p. 186.
46 Turgenev, *Sobranie sochinienii* in 10 volumes (1962), vol. 7, p. 251.
47 Flaubert, II, p. 442.
48 Flaubert, III, p. 68.
49 Turgenev, *Pol. sob. pisem*, XIII (ii), p. 76.
50 Flaubert, I, p. 200.
51 Flaubert, III, p. 306.
52 K. Leontiev, 'Stranitzy Vospominanii' quoted in A. Ostrovsky *Turgenev v zapiskakh sovremennikov* (1929), p. 121.
53 The words of Jules, hero of the first (1845) *Sentimental Education*.
54 I. Howe, *Politics and the Novel* (1957), p. 118.
55 Flaubert, VI, p. 347.
56 Turgenev, *Pol. sob. pisem*, X, p. 183.
57 Turgenev, X, p. 190.
58 Turgenev, X, p. 192.
59 Turgenev, X, p. 194.
60 Turgenev, X, p. 244.
61 Turgenev, *Pol. sob. soch.*, XIV, p. 306.
62 Letters to Julian Schmidt, William Ralston, Ludwig Pietsch, Paul Lindau, Heinrich Laube; *Pol. sob. pisem*, X, pp. 216–7.
63 Flaubert, VII, p. 140.
64 Turgenev, *Pol. sob. pisem*, X, p. 326.
65 Flaubert, I, pp. 185 and 194.

66 Pavlovsky, *Souvenirs*, p. 215.
67 Turgenev, *Pol. sob. soch.*, IX, p. 170.
68 This letter was an angry response on Flaubert's part to the steadfast refusal of the Municipal Council of Rouen to erect a monument to his friend and fellow writer Louis Bouilhet, who died in 1869.
69 Quoted from *Par les champs et par les grèves* (1908), p. 61.
70 Turgenev, *Pol. sob. pisem*, I, p. 279.
71 Flaubert, V, p. 385.
72 Turgenev, *Pol. sob. pisem*, I, p. 355.
73 Turgenev, VIII, p. 272.
74 Flaubert, VI, p. 145.
75 Flaubert, VI, p. 142.
76 Turgenev, *Pol. sob. pisem*, VII, p. 274.
77 Turgenev, VII, p. 284.
78 Flaubert, VI, p. 184.
79 Flaubert, VI, p. 224.
80 Turgenev, *Pol. sob. pisem*, IX, p. 50.
81 Turgenev, IX, p. 71.
82 Pavlovsky, *Souvenirs*, p. 215.
83 Princess Mathilde, 'Gustave Flaubert' in *Gustave Flaubert, Lettres inédites à la princesse Mathilde* (1927).
84 P. Bourget, *Nouveaux essais de psychologie contemporaine* (1885), p. 212.
85 Turgenev, *Pol. sob. soch.*, IX, p. 122.
86 A. Thorlby, *Gustave Flaubert and the Art of Realism* (1956), p. 55.
87 Flaubert, V, p. 158.
88 Turgenev, *Pol. sob. soch.*, VII, p. 50.
89 Flaubert, *La Tentation de Saint Antoine* (Conard edn), p. 207.
90 Flaubert, I, p. 191.
91 Flaubert, II, p. 394.
92 Turgenev, *Pol. sob. pisem*, II, p. 305.
93 Flaubert, VII, p. 294.
94 Flaubert, VII, p. 203.
95 Turgenev, *Pol. sob. soch.*, XIII, p. 205.
96 Flaubert, *Corresp.*, VI, p. 441.
97 Flaubert, *Corresp. supp.*, III, p. 80.
98 R. Wellek, *Concepts of Criticism* (1963), p. 240.
99 Flaubert, *Corresp.*, II, p. 255.
100 *L'Illustration*, 19 July 1845.
101 Turgenev, *Pol. sob. pisem*, XI, p. 31.
102 Flaubert, *Corresp. supp.*, IV, p. 181.
103 Turgenev, *Pol. sob. pisem*, I, p. 292.
104 Flaubert, *Corresp.*, III, p. 163.
105 Flaubert, V, p. 111.
106 Flaubert, III, p. 61.
107 Flaubert, V, p. 228.
108 R. Freeborn, 'Trends of development in the Russian nineteenth-century realistic novel (1830–80)', D. Phil, thesis, Oxford, 1958, p. 230.

109 Bourget, *Nouveaux essais*, p. 215.
110 Turgenev, *Pol. sob. pisem*, XII (ii), p. 327.
111 Flaubert, III, p. 21.
112 Flaubert, VII, p. 331.
113 Turgenev, *Pol. sob. soch.*, XIV, p. 97.
114 Turgenev, *Pol. sob. pisem*, X, p. 49.
115 Flaubert, VII, p. 281.
116 Flaubert, III, p. 281.
117 Flaubert, III, p. 317.
118 Flaubert, IV, p. 136.
119 Turgenev, *Pol. sob. soch.*, VIII, p. 9.
120 Turgenev, *Pol. sob. pisem*, I, p. 389.
121 Turgenev, IV, p. 184.
122 Turgenev, *Pol. sob. soch*, I, p. 227.
123 Flaubert, V, p. 45.
124 Flaubert, III, p. 322.
125 Flaubert, V, p. 179.
126 Flaubert, III, p. 291.
127 G. de Maupassant, 'Souvenirs d'un après-midi chez Gustave Flaubert', *Le Gaulois*, 23 August 1880.

Textual note on the Letters

Full details of these and other editions are given in the Bibliography.

I March 1863—April 1872

1 E. and J. de Goncourt, *Journal – Mémoires de la vie littéraire*, ed. R. Ricatte, VI, p. 36.
2 Ivan Tourguénev, *Nouvelle Correspondance inédite*, ed. A. Zviguilsky, I (1971), pp. 138–9.
3 Flaubert, *Corresp.*, V, p. 368.
4 *Scènes de la vie russe* [*Scenes from Russian life*], translated by M. Marmier (1858) and *Dmitri Roudine*, suivi d'*Un journal d'un homme de trop* et de *Trois rencontres* [*Rudin* followed by the *Diary of a Superfluous Man* and *Three Encounters*], translated by L. Viardot (1862).
5 *Nouvelles scènes de la vie russe* [*New Scenes from Russian Life*] translated by H. Delaveau (1863) and *Les Pères et les Enfants* [*Fathers and Children*] with an introduction by Mérimée (1863).
6 See note 4 above.
7 See note 4 above.
8 The heroine of *On the Eve*. This was included in the volume *Nouvelles scènes de la vie russe*.
9 *Fathers and Children* (see note 5 above).

10   This date (20 March) must be an error on Flaubert's part, as the letter is clearly an answer to Turgenev's dated 18 April 1863.

11   It is clear from a letter Turgenev wrote to Mme Viardot on 29 May 1866 that he had seen Flaubert recently in Paris (Touriguénev, *Nouvelle correspondance*, p. 138).

12   It is not possible to identify the beautiful lady referred to here. Théophile Gautier (1811–72) was a close friend of Flaubert, poet of the romantic movement, and proponent of the theory of art for art's sake. Ernest Renan (1823–92), historian and critic, was much admired by Flaubert. His spiritual crisis of the 1840s made him adopt a 'scientific' and historical approach to religion, revealed in his multi-volume *Les Origines du Christianisme*, written over a period of some twenty years.

13   *Fumée* [*Smoke*] (1868).

14   *Sentimental Education*.

15   Turgenev's illegitimate daughter by his mother's seamstress. She was sent to France at the age of eight to be brought up, at Turgenev's request, with the Viardot children; she was renamed Pauline. The child found it difficult to adjust, and her relationship with her father was never a very close one.

16   Princess Mathilde, a niece of Napoleon Bonaparte, enjoyed an influential position during the reign of her cousin Napoleon III. Her salon in Paris was amongst the most notable of the period; she also entertained writers and artists at her country house at Saint-Gratien.

17   Maxime Du Camp (1822–94), journalist and novelist; he and Flaubert had been close friends as younger men and travelled much together, first in Brittany and then in the Middle East. In later years, they drifted apart.

18   Possibly a reference to *Fumée* [*Smoke*].

19   Charles Augustin Sainte-Beuve (1804–69), literary critic and largely responsible in France for the elevation of literary criticism to a major art form in its own right.

20   This research was in connection with the affairs of the Dambreuse and Arnoux families in *Sentimental Education*.·

21   Hippolyte Taine (1828–93), philosopher and historian; much influenced by positivism, he sought to apply scientific principles to the study of literature, history and art.

22   La Harpe was an eighteenth-century literary critic of the dogmatic school.

23   Jules Husson wrote under the *nom de plume* Champfleury; his wife (sometimes familiarly referred to as La Moutonne) was the mistress of Maxime Du Camp.

24   The journal that Turgenev is referring to here is in fact *The European Messenger*.

25   *Sentimental Education*.

26   An episode in *Sentimental Education*.

27   Lévy had published all of Flaubert's works until this date.

28   'Books have a destiny of their own.'

29 Louis Bouilhet, the poet, a native of Rouen and close friend of Flaubert, died in July 1869.

30 'Man should be fierce.'

31 Turgenev's 'Histoire étrange' ['A Strange Story'] was published in the *Revue des Deux Mondes* on 1 March 1870.

32 Jules Duplan, friend and longstanding correspondent of Flaubert, the brother of his Rouen lawyer.

33 Ernest Feydeau had been a friend of Flaubert's since the late 1850s; he dabbled in the study of ancient cultures, and liked to think that he had provided inspiration for *Salammbô*.

34 Lassouche was a well-known actor.

35 The plebiscite of 8 May 1870 on the question of the setting up of democratically elected institutions within the framework of the Second Empire.

36 A verse drama by Louis Bouilhet.

37 Flaubert had seen the false newspaper reports of the death of Pauline Viardot.

38 Flaubert's answer to Turgenev's letter of 6 May 1871 has unfortunately not survived. The 'events' referred to here are presumably the suppression of the Paris Commune.

39 A satirical journal.

40 Troppmann was a murderer whose trial had excited public opinion. (Turgenev had been present at his execution and wrote an account of his impressions in his *Literary Reminiscences*.)

41 *The Times* confused Ivan Turgenev with his uncle Nicholas (whose death Turgenev refers to in the preceding letter to Flaubert) and declared the novelist to have died at the age of 81.

42 The Viardots were political opponents of the Empire, thus Turgenev wished to keep secret the fact that he frequented the salon of Princess Mathilde, whom they considered as an enemy.

43 The reason for Flaubert's distress at this time was the death of his mother, which occurred on 6 April 1872.

44 Louis Viardot *Merveilles de la peinture*, (1872).

II June 1872–September 1875

1 Turgenev, *Pol. sob. pisem*, XI, p. 109.

2 Turgenev, XI, p. 128.

3 Pierre de Ronsard (1524–85), Renaissance poet and native of Vendôme, much admired by Flaubert.

4 Monseigneur Dupanloup, Bishop of Orleans, theologian and educationalist, who was active in the public debate that preceded the Third Republic's educational reforms.

5 Turgenev considerably enlarged his collection of paintings at this time. This reference is to Blanchard's 'Courtesan', exhibited at the 1872 Salon.

6 In June and July 1872, the French government made two issues of loan stock in order to pay off war indemnities to Prussia ahead of schedule.

7 *L'Homme femme*, Alexandre Dumas the younger's contribution to the debate on whether adulteresses should be killed or pardoned. He favoured the former solution.

8 Théophile Gautier died on 23 October 1872.

9 Sardou, Offenbach and Vacquerie were all writers of comedies.

10 A euphemism for *merde*, shit.

11 Jules Simon (1814–96), Minister of Education and head of the government in 1876.

12 *Mlle de la Quintinie.*

13 For security reasons, the French Assembly had met at Versailles since the Commune of 1871.

14 Badinguet was a popular nickname for Napoleon III, who died in January 1873 in exile at Chislehurst, Kent.

15 Théophile Gautier.

16 A reference to the salon of Princess Mathilde and the fact that Turgenev wished to keep secret from the Viardots his frequentation of supporters of the Empire.

17 The collection of short stories *Histoires étranges* [*Dream Tales*] (1873).

18 *The Weaker Sex* was an unfinished verse drama by Louis Bouilhet that Flaubert undertook to complete and prepare for production.

19 This is a reference to Flaubert's own play *Le Château des Coeurs*.

20 *Les Eaux printanières* [*Spring Torrents*] (1873).

21 Carvalho was Director of the Vaudeville theatre, and Raoul-Duval was Deputy for the Seine-Inférieure.

22 Bouvard and Pécuchet.

23 'True praise is that given by a praiseworthy man.'

24 William Henry Bullock, journalist. His uncle's estate was in Cambridgeshire. Turgenev did not in fact make the projected journey.

25 Gaultier d'Aulnay is one of the victims of intrigue in Alexandre Dumas the elder's medieval play *La Tour de Nesle* of 1832.

26 Patrice Macmahon, who had been a general in the Franco-Prussian War, was elected President of the Third Republic by the Assembly in November 1873, in succession to Thiers.

27 *Rabagas*, a political comedy also by Victorien Sardou, performed in 1872; the current production was his *Uncle Sam*.

28 A play by Sardou.

29 Perrin was administrator of the Comédie-Française.

30 Turgenev negotiated a contract with Stasyulevich for Zola to contribute articles regularly to *The European Messenger*.

31 The name Decius is synonymous with devotion and self-sacrifice in Roman history, from the fourth century BC general, Decius Mus.

32 *Les Héritiers Rabourdin.*

33 This story appeared in the *Revue des Deux Mondes*, vol. 5 (1874).

34 A quotation from Dumas's *Tour de Nesle*. (See note 25 above.)

35 Paul Lindau, German literary critic and friend of Turgenev, wrote three articles on Flaubert's *Temptation of Saint Anthony*.

36 The death of Napoleon III left the Imperial family without an obvious head, his son Louis, the prince Imperial, being a minor. Jérome, the Prince Napoleon and brother of Princess Mathilde, was pretender to the position.

37 Marshal Bazaine, who had been imprisoned in the fortress of the Île Ste Marguerite, escaped on 10 August 1874.

38 In fact *The Weaker Sex* was never performed.

39 The dating of this letter is problematical. Gérard-Gailly dates it 1875 on the grounds that this was the last winter season in which Flaubert maintained a separate establishment from the Commanvilles in Paris.

40 Stories by George Sand.

41 This letter refers to a clandestine performance of Guy de Maupassant's unpublishable and obscene play *A la feuille de rose, Maison turque*.

42 Georges Pouchet, native of Rouen, doctor of science and naturalist.

III October 1875–Spring 1878

1 Turgenev had a chalet built for himself in the grounds of the Viardots' villa at Bougival. It opened as Le Musée Tourguéneff in 1983.

2 Jeokhanan is a reference to the third of Flaubert's short stories, *Hérodias*. The 'old woman' is Félicité, the heroine of *Un Coeur simple* [*A Simple Soul*].

3 Mme Brainne, daughter of a former editor of a Rouen newspaper, was a woman of considerable beauty, and often referred to in Flaubert's correspondence of the mid 1870s as one of his angels.

4 E. Renan, *Dialogues et fragments philosophiques* (1876).

5 George Sand died on 8 June 1876.

6 On 15 June 1876, a Turkish army officer, Hassan, assassinated both the Minister of War and the Minister for Foreign Affairs in Istanbul.

7 A journalist covering G. Sand's funeral for *Le Figaro*.

8 Nephew of Napoleon Bonaparte and brother of the Princess Mathilde.

9 *Dialogues et fragments philosophiques*.

10 E. Fromentin, *Les Maîtres d'autrefois* (1876).

11 Stéphane Mallarmé (1842–98), symbolist poet, had published his famous *Après-midi d'un faune* the previous year.

12 This is a reference to the notorious Eastern question: the instability in South Eastern Europe occasioned by pressure from its neighbours on the declining Ottoman Turkish Empire.

13 This letter is written on pink paper, embossed with an elaborate art nouveau style motif.

14 'Parrot' is a reference to Flaubert's story *A Simple Soul*.

15 Alphonse Daudet, *Fromont jeune et Risler aîné*, written in collaboration with A. Belot and performed at the Vaudeville on 18 September 1876.

16 This study, entitled 'M. Gustave Flaubert', appeared on 22 October 1876 under the pseudonym of Guy de Valmont. [Gérard-Gailly's note.]

17 Maupassant's *A la feuille de rose*.

18   E. de Goncourt, *La Fille Elisa* (1877).
19   Russia, in expansionist mood, was indeed at war with Turkey from 1877 to 1878.
20   Cathos and Madelon are characters in Molière's *Les Précieuses ridicules*.
21   E. Renan, 'Prière sur l'Acropole', *Revue des Deux Mondes*, December 1876.
22   The Comte de Germiny, son of a former governor of the Bank of France, had been arrested, after a struggle, in a public lavatory on the Champs-Elysées.
23   Flaubert's neologism.
24   Catulle-Mendès, *Justice*.
25   Turgenev's story 'The Dream' was published in French translation in *Le Temps* of 20 and 21 January 1877.
26   *Virgin Soil.*
27   Chamerot was the printer responsible for producing Flaubert's *Three Tales*; he was married to one of the Viardot daughters.
28   Saint-Saëns' opera *Le Timbre d'argent* was first performed at the Théâtre lyrique in February 1877.
29   Massenet's opera *Le Roi de Lahore* had its first night in April 1877.
30   Flaubert had known Jeanne de Tourbey since the days when he was working on *Madame Bovary*; he admired her beauty and frequented her brilliant literary salon.
31   Salicylate is a basic component of aspirin.
32   The Russo-Turkish War.
33   Émile Zola's 'Une Histoire d'amour' appeared in *L'Echo Universel* on 27 April 1877.
34   Daudet's *Le Nabab* was serialised in *Le Temps* between 12 July and 21 October 1877.
35   Mme Gras, a widow who blinded her young lover with sulphuric acid in order to obtain administration of his considerable fortune. The case came up for trial in July 1877.
36   It has not been possible to see the manuscript of this letter, which remains in a private collection. It was first published by Gérard-Gailly who was obliged to accept an expurgated version.
37   Thiers, who had been elected president of the Third Republic in 1871, finishing his career as Deputy for Paris, died on 3 September 1877.
38   'Between ourselves, it is on account of Venus!!'
39   *Le Nabab.*
40   Octave Feuillet (1821–90) was a writer of sentimental and romantic novels.
41   Bayard was a fifteenth-century captain whose bravery caused him to be known as 'the fearless and irreproachable knight'; this was Flaubert's ironical nickname for Macmahon.
42   Despite a republican victory in the October elections, Macmahon still prevaricated over the appointment of a republican cabinet and it was not until 13 December that he finally capitulated.
43   In a speech of December 1876, Jules Simon had declared: 'We are

profoundly republican and profoundly conservative' (*Journal des Débats*, 16 December 1876).

44 In *Le Bien Public*, 13 January 1878.

45 N.V. Khanikov (1822–78), émigré Russian geographer and ethnographer, and friend of Turgenev.

46 Guy de Maupassant and Mme Pasca, an actress at the Gymnase theatre.

47 Mme Mazeline was another attractive woman whose company Flaubert enjoyed at his friends' dinner tables.

IV June 1878–May 1880

1 Turgenev participated in the Congrès Littéraire International de Paris in June 1878, under the presidency of Victor Hugo.

2 Henri Martin, the historian, was elected to the Académie Française to fill the vacant seat left by the death of Thiers.

3 A comic opera by Catulle-Mendès, based on Théophile Gautier's novel of the same name, performed at the Théâtre lyrique on 2 July 1878.

4 Mme Régnier was a literary lady who wrote under the pseudonym of Daniel Darc; this note is presumably an answer to a question of Turgenev's in a letter that has been lost.

5 The Père-Lachaise cemetery is in north-east Paris.

6 Sarah Bernhardt, *Dans les Nuages* [*Among the Clouds*] (1878). This work describes a balloon flight the actress made with the painter Clairin.

7 Molière, *Le Malade imaginaire*.

8 A reference to a campaign against Zola started in *Le Figaro* of 15 December 1878 and taken up subsequently in the *Bibliothèque et revue suisse*.

9 Possibly Louis Viardot's *La Science et la Conscience* (1873).

10 Villemessant was editor of *Le Figaro*.

11 'Whether you will it or no.'

12 Jules Ferry, a staunch Republican deputy, became a member of the government in 1879.

13 Flaubert had known Edmond Laporte since the mid-1860s. He was a neighbour and local industrialist, but with literary aspirations.

14 Mme Edmond Adam (Juliette Lamber), editor of *La Nouvelle Revue*, mistress of Gambetta, also maintained a brilliant political and artistic salon.

15 Jules Grévy became President of the Republic in 1879.

16 De Sacy held the post of librarian at the Bibliothèque Mazarine.

17 Mme Pelouze was a highly cultured lady living near Chenonceaux; Flaubert felt awkward in his dealings with her, as he had turned to her for help at the time of his nephew's bankruptcy, but without success.

18 This letter is reproduced in entirety for the first time here.

19 There had been an outbreak of plague in Russia.

20 An anonymous satirical article describing Turgenev's fruitless visit to Mme Adam's salon appeared in *Le Figaro* of 15 February 1879.

21   Caroline Commanville had submitted a painting for the 1879 Salon.
22   Turgenev had wished to send these Swedish fish as a thankyou gift for hospitality received at Croisset.
23   Gérard-Gailly dates this letter December 1879, but as Flaubert thanks Turgenev for his Christmas parcels of salmon and caviar in two other letters, this one would seem to be a reference to the two pounds of Swedish fish and to Turgenev's visit to Croisset in the first week of May 1879.
24   Turgenev's visit to England in June 1879 was in order to receive an honorary doctorate conferred on him by the University of Oxford.
25   In the summer of 1879, Turgenev received an honour from the French government; he was made an Officier de l'instruction publique.
26   Turgenev's short story 'Monsieur François' was published in *La Nouvelle Revue* on 15 December 1879.
27   A. Daudet, *Les rois en exil*; the first instalment appeared in *Le Temps* on 15 August 1879.
28   *Nana* by Émile Zola.
29   E. Renan, *L'Eglise chrétienne*, vol. 6 of *L'Histoire des origines du Christianisme*, was published in October 1879.
30   'Where many things shine in a poem.'
31   Marietta Alboni (1824–94) was a well-known Italian operatic singer.
32   Turgenev's friend Isaac Pavlovsky published a piece entitled 'En Cellule' in *Le Temps* on 12 November 1879.
33   The sculptor Pradier who worked on the tomb of Napoleon Bonaparte.
34   Flaubert needed some botanical details for *Bouvard and Pécuchet*. A professor at the Jardin des Plantes in Paris had confirmed Flaubert's own *intuitive* notion over the view of Baudry, a local Rouen naturalist.

Bibliography

Editions of Turgenev's correspondence

Polnoe sobranie sochinenii i pisem, Soviet Academy of Sciences, 12 vols, (Moscow, 1961–8).
Tourguéneff and his French circle, ed. E. Halpérine-Kaminsky, trs. E.M. Arnold (London, 1898).
Ivan Tourguéneff d'après sa correspondance avec ses amis français, ed. E. Halpérine-Kaminsky Paris, 1901).
Ivan Tourguénev: Lettres inédites à Pauline Viardot et à sa famille. ed. H. Granjard and A. Zviguilsky (Paris 1972).
Ivan Tourguénev: Nouvelle correspondance inédite, ed. A. Zviguilsky, 2 vols (Paris, 1971).
Turgenev's Letters, ed. A.V. Knowles (London, 1983).
Selected Letters of Ivan Turgenev, ed. D. Lowe, 2 vols (Ann Arbor, Michigan, (1983).

Editions of Flaubert's correspondence

Correspondance – nouvelle édition, 9 vols, Conard (Paris, 1926–33).
Lettres inédites à Tourguéneff, ed. Gerard-Gailly (Monaco, 1946).
Correspondance – supplément, 4 vols, Conard (Paris, 1954).
Oeuvres complètes, 16 vols, Club de l'honnête homme (Paris, 1972).
Correspondance, Bibliothèque de la Pléiade (Paris, vol I, 1973; vol II, 1980).
The Letters of Gustave Flaubert, ed. F. Steegmuller, 2 vols, (Cambridge, Mass., 1980–82).

Works consulted in the preparation of this edition

Albalat, A., *Gustave Flaubert et ses amis* (Paris, 1927).
Baldick, R., *Dinner at Magny's* (London, 1971).
Bourget, P., *Nouveaux essais de psychologie contemporaine* (Paris, 1885).
Carlut, C., *La correspondance de Flaubert – étude et répertoire critique* (Paris, 1968).
Daudet, Mme A., *Souvenirs autour d'un groupe littéraire* (Paris, 1910).
Daudet, A., *Trente ans de Paris* (Paris, 1888).
Digeon, C., *Le dernier visage de Flaubert*, (Paris, 1946).
Fitzlyon, A., *The Price of Genius: The life of Pauline Viardot* (London, 1964).

Freeborn, R., *Turgenev: The novelist's novelist* (Oxford, 1960).

de Goncourt, E. and J., *Journal – mémoires de la vie littéraire*, ed. R. Ricatte, 22 vols (Monaco, 1956–8).

Howe, I., *Politics and the Novel* (New York, 1957).

Magarshack, D. (ed.), *Turgenev's Literary Reminiscences* (London, 1959).

de Maupassant, G., *Chroniques, études, correspondances* (Paris, 1938).

Mazon, A., *Manuscrits parisiens d'Ivan Tourguéneff* (Paris, 1930).

Pavlovsky, I., *Souvenirs sur Tourguéneff* (Paris, 1887).

Reik, T., *Flaubert und seine Versuchung des heiligen Antonius: ein Beitrag zur Künstlerpsychologie* (Minden, 1912).

Thorlby, A., *Gustave Flaubert and the Art of Realism* (London, 1956).

Tricotel, C., *Comme deux troubadours – Histoire de l'amitié Flaubert-Sand* (Paris, 1978).

de Vogüé, E.M., *Le Roman russe* (Paris, 1886).

Waddington, P., *Turgenev and George Sand: An improbable entente* (London, 1981).

Wellek, R., *Concepts of Criticism* (London, 1963).

Zola, E., 'Souvenirs contemporains: Flaubert et Tourguéneff', in *Annales Politiques et Littéraires*, 12 November 1893.

Index